ALAN BIGGINS

A
NORMANDY
TAPESTRY

KIRKDALE BOOKS

A Normandy Tapestry.

Alan Biggins moved to France with his wife and children to study French. The job he found to pay for his studies, 'taking on' and selling French property, has taken him behind the scenes of French rural life.

His tales of rural Normandy and its people are set in a landscape which varies from hidden valleys and sunken lanes to the stunning splendour of Mont St Michel. He tells of a land of remote farms and country hospitality, of cider, coffee and calvados. A land rich in wildlife; salamanders and snakes, boars and beech martens, and that strangest of creatures, the 'Bee Jay'.

The book is rich in humorous incidents, such as bartering a bidet for calvados, being tutored in the ways of philosophy and septic tanks, and a meeting with The Six Potato Man. For the would-be buyer there are some cautionary tales.

This book is about a family too: their experiences in settling in, a process that began with a series of (in hindsight) comical disasters. It recounts their trials and triumphs; in school, learning French and socialising. In the background, as always in Normandy, is the song of the sea.

Since man first sailed the Channel, the fates of England and Normandy have been entwined. From Druids to D-Day, here is our shared story.

In bringing these threads together, the author has woven an amusing, informative and atmospheric tapestry of an enchanting area that remains, in the words of many of its English visitors 'like England when I was a child'.

FOR
Alan & Molly Waters
and their children.

Published by KIRKDALE BOOKS
Great Horwood,
Milton Keynes,
Buckinghamshire.

First published: April 1994
ISBN 0-9523149-0-8

Made and printed in Great Britain by
Cromwell Press,
Melksham.
Photoset in Palatino 11/12.

British Library Cataloguing in Publication Data. A
catalogue record is available for this book from the British
Library.

Illustrations: Tony Beesley(cover). Erica Stokes. Bridie
Fisher. Ann Biggins.

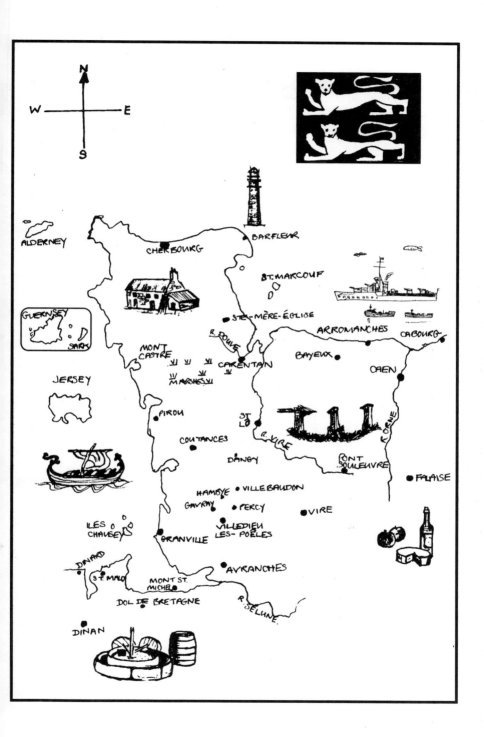

ALDERNEY

CHERBOURG BARFLEUR

ST.MARCOUF

GUERNSEY
SARK

STE-MÈRE-ÉGLISE ARROMANCHES CABOURG

R. DOUVE

MONT CASTRE BAYEUX CAEN

JERSEY CARENTAN

MARSHES

PIROU ST LO

COUTANCES R. VIRE

DANGY PONT SOULEUVRE

HAMBYE VILLEBAUDON FALAISE

GAVRAY PERCY VIRE

ILES O CHAUSEY VILLEDIEU LES-POÊLES

GRANVILLE

DINARD AVRANCHES

ST. MALO

MONT ST. MICHEL

DOL DE BRETAGNE R. SÉLUNE

DINAN

CONTENTS.

Teething troubles. Two whistling builders.
We begin to learn.

I stopped the car in front of the grey Norman farmhouse, switched off the engine and kissed Ann.

"Here's to luck in our new home."

Alice and David were asleep under a pile of coats in the back of our faithful old Vauxhall estate. From somewhere in the mound behind them, there came a plaintive 'miaow'.

It was the ninth of January. The house looked sadder than it had the previous year. Perhaps it was the mist that swirled in the orchard, maybe it was the bareness of the trees; or it could have been that the place, shuttered up, looked blind. Never mind. It would be spring soon. The first green shoots of the daffodil bulbs we had planted back in September were already showing through the grass.

The key was under a flowerpot and, after a little persuasion from my shoulder, we entered our new home. A fire was laid in the living room. I put a match to it.

"Open the shutters," commanded Ann. "Let's get some daylight in the place!"

I did as I was told. Mounds of dead flies covered the window sills but otherwise the house had been left spotlessly clean. The children ran about the big old place.

"Careful on the stone floors, children!" counselled their mother. "Careful on the wooden stairs! Why aren't you wearing your slippers?"

But it's difficult to hold a seven-year-old and a four-year-old in check, especially when they have the excitement of a new home to explore. Alice won the argument over bedrooms ("I am the oldest you know!"), bagging the room overlooking the front door as being the best place from which to ambush visitors with her water pistol. David had to be content with what he got.

Ann busied herself with the camping gas stove as I began to unload the car. Hardly had we finished our first cup of tea than we had our first visitor. He was a tall man of around sixty with a weather-beaten face and a cloth cap, who introduced himself as Albert, our next-door neighbour. Would we care to visit him for coffee? Yes, very much. Within a few minutes the four of us were ranged along a wooden bench at an oil-cloth-covered farmhouse table, being plied with coffee, calvados and sweets. A wood stove burned merrily in the background.

The conversation was rather stilted. In those days our French was hesitant and the children's non-existent. It didn't matter. It was obvious that we had good neighbours. The time came to leave.

"If you need anything, don't hesitate to call." I took Albert's phrase to be a mere formality. I thanked him for the offer, not imagining how soon we would need his help.

The furniture van arrived shortly afterwards and Wayne and Gareth began the serious business of unpacking, slightly impeded by Alice and David scuttling in and out. "Don't get in the way children. Sit by the fire!" Mounds of boxes and pieces of furniture soon began to pile up. One wardrobe was too big for the stairs but the lads didn't turn a hair. Within a couple of minutes it had disappeared up a ladder and through the only upstairs window without a bar across it (the bars being to stop people falling out, rather than to keep them in). I busied myself changing English electrical plugs for French ones. The short winter day came to an end and the fog swirled closer to the house.

CLACK!

With a sound as of a giant mousetrap snapping shut, we were plunged into darkness. The six of us froze in mid movement, stranded; Ann in the kitchen, the children by the fire, I with my screwdriver and plug, Wayne and Gareth half-way between removal van and house.

"Bloody hell!" said Wayne. I groped my way to the car and positioned it so that the headlights shone into the house. Ann produced a torch from somewhere. Then I searched out the junction box and re-set the main trip-switch. Light was restored. A cup of tea was needed. Ann turned on a tap. A mere drop of water:

CLACK!

With a four-year-old and a seven-year-old, in the depths of a winter's night, and with half of our worldly goods (including the beds) still in the lorry outside, the situation was far from amusing. It was hardly the moment to embark on a crash course on French electricity but that was what I must do. Our neighbour had told us to ask for help if we had problems. We had problems.

Albert didn't seem to mind being pulled away from his television. He looked musingly at the electrics and reset the trip-switch, which he told me was called the disjoncteur. It tripped out again. I mentioned that our problems had begun when Ann had turned the tap on.

"C'est la pompe," he nodded thoughtfully.

What had a pump got to do with our problems?

"Le pwee." Albert continued obscurely. I was still mystified: what was a pwee? He led me outside and pointed to a square inspection hatch in the centre of a large concrete cover set into

11

the grass. It was no stranger to me: I had lifted it off in September and stared thoughtfully into the dark depths. There was water down there. I had assumed it to be the Fosse Septique (septic tank). It was not. It was le pwee ...of course, it was a well - un puit! La pompe which raised the water from le puit had failed and le disjoncteur had disjoncted.

We went back indoors and played the torch over the neatly labelled row of fuses. With a grunt of satisfaction, Albert removed the one marked 'pompe' and reset the disjoncteur. Light! But no water. Pas de probleme! With a variety of pans, buckets and bottles, father, mother, son and daughter followed Albert home.

Eventually the unloading was done and Wayne and Gareth left. It was time to get the children ready for bed. The fire had gone out by now and it was deadly cold everywhere. We switched on several electric radiators.

CLACK!

The metallic sound echoed through the house with the finality of the crack of doom. Darkness.

"Mummy! Daddy!" The children were scared now. They called to us softly from their rooms. Uprooted from their predictable English life and hustled abroad like spare luggage, nothing in their ordered existence had prepared them for this. Ann and I were twitchy too. We hadn't expected a red carpet on arriving in France; on the other hand we had not bargained on the very forces of nature making sport of us. Could this be natural, or had we overstepped some unseen mark? The only thing that was missing was the jagged music from 'Psycho'.

Putting aside the thought, I went to do battle with the disjoncteur. I switched it on. It switched itself off.

"Damn you!"

On. Off. I used stronger Anglo-Saxon words. I did not have the vocabulary to curse it in French. Perhaps it was overloaded? Very well, we must turn off some radiators.

12

OF PUMPS, POWER, AND POUTRES.

CLACK!

It took several 'disjoncts' before we learned that the maximum number of radiators our disjoncteur would tolerate was three. The house has ten of them.

The children insisted on sleeping in our bed. "Should I have drawn a pentagram around them?" asked Ann as we huddled glumly over the little gas stove.

Then the doorbell rang. What now? I had had a great deal of trouble closing the door after Wayne and Gareth, for the house had lain empty for eighteen months and damp had caused the woodwork to swell. After a series of desperate tugs which all but pulled the handle off, I wrenched the thing open. Fists clenched tight, I glowered into the freezing fog. What would I see? A mad axeman? The Grim Reaper? It didn't matter. I was ready for them. "Welcome to France." The two neatly dressed middle-aged ladies spoke a little uncertainly.

Hastily recomposing my cheeks, lips and teeth into the nearest approach to a smile that I could manage, I invited them in. Ann gave me a surprisingly sour look. In halting French I offered them tea and thanked them for coming to welcome us.

They were Jehovah's witnesses. One of the pair had lapsed from just about every faith known to man. Jehovah was her twelfth religion. We admired her honesty in owning up to past mistakes, but felt that her track record left something to be desired. Finally we got rid of them and searched out our own spiritual solace.

In one short day we had gone from a comfortable Buckinghamshire village and a cosy end-of-terrace with double glazing, central heating and fully-fitted Coronation Street, to a fog-shrouded Norman farmhouse watched over by the crazed deities of French electrics and water. Playthings of the pompe! Dupes of the disjoncteur! Legitimate prey for Holy Rollers! We looked at each other in silence. What on earth had we let ourselves in for?

Over the road from our house is the farm of our other neighbours in the hamlet, René and Therese. We met them on the second day. They were a God-send, for wood to begin with. Stone houses are like giant storage heaters which take in and release heat very slowly. They remain cool in summer but are a devil to heat up from scratch. René supplied us with logs from his wood pile so that we could at least keep one room warm.

We still, of course, had our little problem with the pump. No water means no toilet. Worse, it means no tea. I tied a towing rope to a five gallon plastic bucket and dropped it down the well. It floated, so I weighted it down with a stone and tried again. Then I hauled the water thirty feet up the well (after two summers of drought, the water level was very low), staggered into the house with it and did the necessary.

We asked Albert what he thought our next move should be. "I'll 'phone Jean," he said briefly. Jean (the previous owner of the house) arrived half an hour later. A farmer of about my own age, he rolled the concrete cover off the well as easily as if it had been a Camembert cheese and fished out the pump. Perhaps it was a short circuit? He stripped back the wires with a penknife (all French countrymen seem to carry penknives and baler twine) and reassembled the connection box. No go. He 'phoned the water board; there was a newly arrived family without water. He turned to us sadly.

"I am desolated, but they say that as the house is on well-water it's not their problem ...though they will connect you up given time, say five weeks."

Meanwhile we would have to get by. There seemed little alternative but to order a new pump.

"It was on the mains once," Jean explained, "but the pipes burst during the big freeze of eighty-four. I never did like the mains, tastes of chemicals if you ask me" - his face broke into a radiant smile - "so I took the opportunity of switching to well-water. It is beautiful."

Then and there we made a vow to put the house back onto

the mains.

The pump arrived five days later. Our resolution to re-connect to the mains was strengthened with its fitting. This was partly because it would only deliver water upstairs if a tap was first turned on downstairs, and partly because of the unexpected effect it had on the electrical supply. When a tap was turned on and the pump cut in, all the lights in the house dimmed. It was like being in a submarine under attack.

They say that troubles, like buses, come in threes. Certainly that was the way of it for us in Normandy. After the pump and the power supply we were confronted with the third of the evil spirits that inhabited our house - la poutre (the beam). The floors in Alice's bedroom and the bathroom, and the corridor between them, had a curiously springy feel, as though they lacked support. Investigation revealed that the level of the bathroom floor was an inch below the bottom of the skirting board.

I rang up the agency through which we had bought the house. They were sorry to hear of our problems, but could recommend a very good English builder who would be able to sort it out.

The arrival of the builder heralded the opening of round three: Biggins versus the poutre. The builder poked a stick into the gap between the bathroom floor and skirting board and whistled thoughtfully. Then he went downstairs and looked at the two massive oak beams in the ceiling. He drew in his breath, nodded wisely and pointed upwards.

"One of them buggers has shifted. That's why your floor upstairs is on a slant." He stood on a chair, tapped the wall and shook his head gravely. "Cavity wall insulation, that's bad. Hides a multitude of sins does this stuff. It'll all have to be ripped out, then we can jack up the beam by a couple of inches and fix it properly into the walls." His reassuring tone would have done credit to a doctor. "Don't worry Mr Biggins, you've come to the right man. I can get my hands on some really powerful jacks straight away. They'll lift that ceiling, no problem at all. When do you want me to start?"

Massive jacks, creaking cogs, slow moving ratchets, shifting beams, toppling walls, dust and debris. It conjured up visions of The Temple of Doom in our own living room. We wanted a second opinion.

Meanwhile, the children started school. We are a close family, we four, and the strange doings at the house had drawn us closer. If French electricity, water and wood were in such obvious conspiracy against us, was it wise to leave our children to the mercies of their educational system?

David seemed to share our doubts. "I don't like the look of this lot much" was his first comment on his class-mates. They looked perfectly nice children to me but we could sympathise with him. It was his first day of school, a traumatic enough experience at the best of times. Here it was to be with strangers whose language he did not speak.

Alice was not keen either. That the two were at different schools didn't help much, but at least it saved me from seeing the sad scene between David and his mother. Only after promising them that they could come home for lunch did we get them into school. Then we hurried back to the house. We had an appointment with builder number two.

Builder number two was a Frenchman. Laboriously I explained the problem to him. He was a whistler too, and added a new word to our French vocabulary that was to become very familiar with the passing of time. It was 'bizarre'. He looked at the floor and he looked at the ceiling, whistling the while. Then he delivered his verdict: the upstairs' floorboards must be ripped out and new supporting beams laid.

Two whistling builders. Two opinions. It seemed to us that it would be a good idea to know the cause of the problem before trying to cure it. By this time we had our own suspicions. The cavity walling wasn't quite snug against one of the two main beams; could the wood have shrunk? I asked the French builder to telephone Jean. The mystery was explained.

One end of our house had been a barn when Jean bought it. He had converted the lower part of it into a living room, putting in the two massive oak beams to support the floor of the bathroom, bedroom and corridor which he constructed upstairs. Then he had put in cavity wall insulation. He had made a very nice job of it all. Unfortunately he had used unseasoned wood for one of the main beams.

The floors came up, thicker cross beams were laid, and the floors went down again.

Why the Building Inspectorate had not picked up the problem I don't know; probably because it was one that took time to become apparent. The agent from whom we had bought the place had not noticed it because he was not a surveyor ("it's been standing three hundred years, I dare say it'll be good for a few more"). The surveyor had not picked it up because there are no surveys on French properties. We had not picked it up because we had not looked closely enough.

By now it was lunchtime and time to pick up the kids from school. We were dying to know how their first morning had gone. They had a lot to learn. And so, for that matter, did we.

A lonely land in winter. Terror in the Owl House.
A country welcome. Selling dreams.
Farmer Lamache.

I was in France to learn.

I was aiming for the Diploma of the Institute of Linguists, a self-study course. I had eighteen months to prepare for my exams. The job that I was to do - selling houses to the British - would give me plenty of opportunity to practise French as well as help to pay for my studies.

I was to open up a new sales area in the south of the Cherbourg Peninsula in Normandy. It was to be roughly triangular in shape. Two of its 'points', the port of Granville and Mont St Michel, were on the coast. The third was inland at Vire, famous for its chitterlings ("chitterlings: smaller intestines of pig, especially when cooked for food" - Oxford English Dictionary).

It is a gentle, rolling and intensely green countryside, where streams flow through rocky outcrops and lose themselves in the bracken. The fields are small and irregular and are grazed by cows. The underlying rock is granite and the water is beautifully soft.

With its narrow, twisting lanes, unexpected viewpoints and secret valleys, it could just as well be in the West Country as in France. There are thousands of woods, copses and orchards. In Devon they call such land 'bosky', in Normandy 'bocage', which suggests (correctly) that not only are the landscapes strikingly similar but that once, long ago, the same language was spoken on both sides of the Channel.

To the north of the area the land rises to the great forest of Saint Sever, a lonely place of wild boar and secret lakes. To the south west it slopes gently to the coast, giving spectacular views of Mont St Michel and the sea. The towns and villages are small but the countryside is scattered with thousand upon thousand of hamlets. The whole area is criss-crossed by minor roads and tracks. Stone crosses and wayside shrines abound.

Naturally, before you can sell houses, you must have houses to sell. 'Taking on' a suitable stock was to be my first task. There is no lack of empty houses in Normandy: it is part of a vast area of France which is suffering from depopulation. The drift to the towns which took place in Britain in the nineteenth century is still going on and it is not unusual for the population of a commune (parish) to have halved since the War.

The agency for which I was to work already had a few houses in 'my' area. I purchased a stack of large scale 'blue' maps and set off to find them. I quickly became used to driving through villages which were deserted save for the occasional gun-belted policeman operating speed traps and carrying out random document checks.

Previously in France I had always driven a British car and had never been bothered by the police. Nor did I expect to be, having driven for fifteen years in England without once having been pulled up. Driving a French car was to change my expectations. I was stopped three times within the first three months of being in Normandy. "Vos papiers, Monsieur."

On one of these occasions the policeman circled my car and ordered me to turn on all the lights. A rear lamp was defective. Ah! That was interesting! Triumphantly he reached for his book of forms. Then he asked to see my licence. I explained that I didn't have it with me because it was at the DVLC at Swansea. The copper struggled with the notion for a moment, then lost interest. "On your way!" (When I told my neighbour René about this experience he was envious. "No such gifts for the French," he told me.)

I soon learned the first lesson of French estate agency. Good houses sell fast, the bad linger on the books. 'My' houses had come onto the books over a period of five years. There were some strange places. The strangest of all was situated south of Villedieu, which is an area not unlike the lower valleys of Dartmoor. Here abandoned granite quarries are commonplace. In winter it is a sombre and lonely country, a fit setting for 'The Owl House'.

To get to The Owl House, I travelled through a place I will call Tristeville. This village, with its sombre church (rebuilt after the War) and brooding early-warning scanner, could probably carry off the prize for the most eerie settlement in Normandy. The radar 'golf ball' does not have the ethereal beauty of the huge white and pristine 'balls' of Fylingdales on the North Yorkshire moors. It is green, tatty, peeling and stuck on a stick.

Unusually, there was somebody in the streets of Tristeville, an elderly woman dressed in black. The French know their area far better than the English, and I stopped to ask her for directions to The Owl House. At first she was friendly but when I showed her a photograph of the property her attitude changed. She crossed herself and took a step backwards from the car, motioning to a side road as she did so.

"It is up there Monsieur; but nobody goes there now." She turned on her heel and disappeared into a house. It was an ominous introduction - but not an inappropriate one.

After driving for twenty minutes through the shattered land I came upon the house, a cadaverous detached building of four storeys, which stood quite alone. Several of the shutters were broken and the steep roof had shed most of its slates. A stone flight of steps led up to the front door, which was hanging from one hinge.

I entered with some trepidation. In the kitchen a large section of tiling had been smashed from the floor - apparently with a hammer - enabling me to gaze down into the cellar where a disquieting scuffling was to be heard. Wallpaper peeled damply from the walls. Undoubtedly the most valuable items in the house were the old-fashioned porcelain and pleated-string pulleys used to move the light bulbs up and down.

Gingerly I climbed the once beautiful staircase to the next floor. More rooms like the ones below. I prepared to climb higher but the stairs had been boarded up. What lay beyond the barrier; the coffins and shrouds, the victims and blood?

Taking my courage in both hands (It was a January afternoon, coming onto darkness) I went outside to look for the answer. Round the back, a rickety breeze-block staircase led up to an entrance on the third floor. The house had been split into two flats. I climbed up. The door swung open too readily for my liking. The shutters were closed and it was difficult to see in the murk. I found the stairs and climbed to the attic. Half of the slate roof was gone; the two gable ends threatening to collapse at any minute.

As I peered into the darkest corner a pure-white owl exploded out of the blackness, all but knocking me off my feet. I scuttled down the stairs, only pulling myself together when I was outside again. Feeling guilty at my own cowardice, I looked around.

In a ruinous out-building at the rear, I found a pile of eastern literature. The Moonies had been here before me. Across the road was an abandoned stone-mason's yard, choked with shattered debris. Part-finished black granite tombstones littered the plot. With a shock, I noticed among them a figure whom I had not remarked earlier, watching me in silence. I admitted defeat and fled the place in blind terror.

The welcome was a good deal warmer when the houses were occupied. The owners had lived in the same area, often the same house, all of their lives. They were friendly people who, as they say in Yorkshire, had no 'side'. A ritual would take place.

I would be shown round their property and then plied with heart-stoppingly strong black coffee containing a tot of calvados (calvados is distilled cider). It is difficult to refuse the hospitality of a Norman host. Excuses such as driving are not as readily accepted as they are in England (especially by the older generation), while pretending to be on a course of antibiotics merely draws scornful looks.

They were intrigued to meet an Englishman but conversation was far from easy at first. The language was a barrier that I only slowly overcame and some of the country people have such thick Norman accents that even the French have difficulty in understanding them. Thus I would be reduced to a fixed smile and the stock phrase, hoping that the conversation wasn't on the lines of:

(Farmer) "My best cow's got a goitre."

(Self) "Oh yes, that's nice."

(Farmer) "And my wife's run off with the vet."

(Self) "Oh, good." (Accompanied by a sickly grin.)

Not only was I learning French; I was learning my job too. This was by no means as straightforward as I had anticipated. The boss of the agency was semi-retired and could not train me. The other Englishman who already worked there had no time to do so. Nor was he paid to; he, like me, being paid only on sales achieved.

TAKING ON.

Mine was, I was told, purely a sales role. The notaires (solicitors) and the clerk in the front office would deal with the legalities. As far as building matters went, they weren't our field. We were not selling houses, we were selling dreams. If I felt strongly about the matter there was another English agent, Peter Edwards, who knew about such things.

Being expected to assess, value, describe and sell properties worth tens of thousands of pounds, while knowing nothing of building regulations, construction methods, French law, or financial matters, did not appear to me to be an ideal situation, especially in the light of our own recent experiences.

I contacted Peter Edwards and found myself in the somewhat 'bizarre' position of being trained by a rival - free. It was good training too. After half a dozen two-hour sessions with him, I felt much happier.

The agency had advertised in the local newspaper for houses in my area. This gave me several more properties. Soon, however, the supply began to dry up. If I discounted the duds such as the 'Owl House', my property file was still depressingly thin. I intensified my efforts to find more houses: talking to neighbours, putting small adverts in supermarkets, dropping cards through doors and the like.

One of the most promising of these initiatives was a contact with a French builder whom Ann and I had met on a previous visit. His response to my telephone call was enthusiastic.

"Houses, Monsieur? But yes. I know of many houses for sale. I am a builder! Visit me in the morning and I will show you."

I arrived at his house early the next day, to be immediately surrounded by relations and family. I was itching to see the marvellous maisons that the inside knowledge of my friend had uncovered. But it was not to be. One of the many, many things I did not yet know about France was the law of the sacred dejeuner. Briefly stated, this is that if business of any duration is to be conducted, it must begin at two in the afternoon. Therefore I was invited to lunch.

It was a meal fit for a king, or a French family; but it is the drink rather than the food that stays in my memory. Alcohol. As course followed course, the complementary tipple appeared. Each had its place, each its function. Aperitifs, snifters and snorters, bracers and chasers; cider, white wine, red wine, pastis and calvados. Even though I was drinking considerably less than my host, I was slightly squiffy by the end of the meal.

Then it was time to see the houses. It was a cold day with a sky of steel-grey. It would snow soon.

"I will drive!" Said the builder majestically as he reeled to the door. This hardly seemed fair on him, his wife, his children, myself; or indeed on anyone else in that part of Normandy. Gently I insisted on taking my car. To give the fellow his due, he did not argue. He probably would have found it difficult to string the words together.

Beneath the slopes of Cader Idris, in the very fastnesses of Wales, there exists, so it is said, a farm like no other. A farm that does not feature on the Ordnance Survey maps, and where none but the invited have ever penetrated. A farm that is hymned of by the bards of the Eistedfford itself - for on it are bred the finest, the most superb rams in the world. If the least of them were put to another man's ewes, the lucky fellow would double the value of his flock.

At lunch my host had hinted broadly that his houses were the French property equivalent of that farm. Mysterious, undiscovered, inaccessible to the outsider, but rich beyond measure. Surrounded by enchantments and magical mists, they lay forever wreathed from the unbeliever's eye. I had been chosen to see them. Excitement was high.

We got into my car and drove off. My builder directed me to a garage. We parked the car and he preceded me into the reception area, where he seemed on good terms with the staff. He helped himself to a beer from the fridge in the corner and made himself comfortable.

"Now we must wait," he said obscurely. I found this a little odd.

TAKING ON.

Eventually an Englishman arrived with a book of property details. He told me that he worked for an estate agency. His only desire was to help me. He was a very charming man. Nevertheless, it was a delicate situation. I explained hesitantly that somehow there had been a misunderstanding and that I was afraid I was wasting his time. I, too, was an estate agent of sorts.

The change in my erstwhile friend was electric. It was as if he had suddenly noticed that I had his wallet in my hand. The easy geniality died from his face and his eyes became suddenly cold and hard: I have rarely seen a man as angry. This was no Peter Edwards.

"Bastard!" was the kindest adjective that he threw back at me as he marched to his car. He slotted a cassette into the player and turned it to its highest volume. Then, emitting a string of curses mixed with the menacing opening bars of 'Summer in the City', he reversed out of the car park at high speed. Unfortunately for him at too high a speed, for he promptly landed his car in a ditch.

It was a quiet road but within a few minutes half a dozen cars and a tractor had stopped to see what was going on. The French are not like the English; they are accustomed to getting involved in what happens around them.

Under the slightly confusing direction of the builder, a dozen men quickly manhandled the grounded vehicle to safety. Literally purple with rage now, the agent roared off, watched by his bemused (and unthanked) helpers. My friend, still a little the worse for wear, insisted on recounting our business to the small crowd. Slowly they drifted away. All except three.

A sallow man saluted me gravely with a nod. "Perhaps you would be interested to know, Monsieur, that Madame LeBrun, the lady in the chateau, is looking to sell up. She hasn't put the place on the market yet. It is a very fine house."

I was more than interested.

The second driver had a brother-in-law who was trying to get rid of some barns. I made a note of the details.

Finally, I was left with one man. His name was, let us say, Monsieur Lamache. He was a middling-height, bow-legged fellow with a wind (or wine) mottled face, and a little short of his breath. There was something extraordinarily likeable about him. Given a pair of long leather boots, a top-coat, a whip, a stagecoach-and-four and a light sprinkling of snow, he would have made an ideal subject for a christmas card. By the look of the sky, the sprinkling of snow was imminent.

Monsieur Lamache was, he told me, a farmer. His farm was not for sale just yet, but he would be retiring in three months. He had already made a deal to sell his land - was I interested in seeing the house? I was very interested. Now? Yes.

"If Monsieur would care to follow me?" Asked the farmer courteously.

The snow began to fall as I pulled out behind the white Renault van. The windscreen wipers swished monotonously. My builder friend fell asleep in the passenger seat.

Farmer Lamache lived to the north of Mont St Michel, on an isolated headland which is served by few roads and consists of little but salt-marsh and the mud flats of the bay. Curlews wheel and cry above the cold pools. Barren and harsh though they seem, these flats are important farming land, for the lambs that are raised on them are highly prized for their flavour.

Farmer Lamache wanted to retire to a town. His farm buildings were a handsome granite-grey group set around a stackyard. Flanking the house were two large barns, one of which held a miscellany of farm machinery, the other, winter feed. In the centre of the yard was an old-fashioned covered well complete with a windlass. Farmer Lamache was obviously not taking any chances with his 'pompe'.

At the end of one of the barns stood an open-sided building. In it was a huge round granite trough, into which was slotted a wooden-shafted crushing wheel. To this, long ago, dray horses had been chained. Sheltered from sun and rain alike, the gentle giants had patiently trodden through the years, pressing out the cider.

The farmhouse was dignified, long, and had many windows and doors. A round tower, made of clay and culminating in a tiled witches-hat roof, thrust up from one end of it. I would not have been surprised to see Rapunzel pressing her face against the little window under the eaves. Chickens and a cock were scratching in the worm-rich heap. The scene could hardly have changed since perhaps 1650.

Monsieur Lamache spoke in the thickest Norman patois as he escorted me around the house. It had many of the features I was soon to take for granted in Norman houses. The large shadowy rooms had thick stone walls, tiny windows and poor lighting. The floors were of stone or earth on the ground floor, wooden boards upstairs. Not a carpet was to be seen. The furniture was sparse, massive and made of oak. The cupboards and chests were beautiful antiques with lovingly burnished brass fittings.

In the main downstairs rooms were great granite fireplaces, each with a chimney wide enough to take a brace of sweep's boys. A fire burned in one. There was a faint smell of wood smoke. In the hall a distinctively Norman grandfather clock ticked away the centuries. A door in the kitchen gave onto the animals' quarters.

Farmer Lamache explained this and that as we walked around. He had wartime memories, another distinctive feature of the older generation. He stopped at the dairy to show me where the Germans had laid trip-wires before leaving; one end connected to a sliding door, the other to copper tubes packed with explosives. "What does 'booby trap' mean, Monsieur? That's what the Americans wrote on the door."

We went back indoors and sat down to cider. Finally I asked the key question: how much did he want for the house? He muttered something. I repeated the question.

"Seventy bricks."

"Seventy bricks?" I repeated faintly.

"Pardon, Monsieur, I mean seventy million."

Numbers are the hardest part of a foreign language to grasp. The fact that older French people invariably spoke in terms of the old franc (the franc was devalued in 1958 to a hundredth of its former value), was extremely confusing at first. The farmer wanted approximately seven hundred thousand francs - about seventy thousand pounds - for his property.

Farmer Lamache bade me goodbye in the stackyard and abruptly turned his back. At first I thought that something had caught his attention. But no, steam was rising. He was relieving himself on his midden with as little self-consciousness as did his cows, much as Norman farmers have done since long before 1650.

"Ah, are we back so soon?" The builder awoke as I pulled up on the drive of his house. He seemed disorientated and I had the greatest of difficulty in dissuading him from trying to contact other estate agents for me. I felt that he had done me enough of a good turn already. Thanks to him I had seen a 'dream house': and I would soon be taking on several other properties.

GAVRAY MARKET

A small farm in Normandy.
Imperial measures and the Code Napoleon.
Gavray market.

The track up to our neighbour René's farmhouse is across a meadow dotted with apple trees and cows. A flock of hens and guinea-fowl roam unchecked about the place and often out into the road. Usually a couple of massive tree trunks lie under the apple trees, waiting to be split into logs for the fire. Wood is a serious business in Normandy.

If any stranger approaches the farm a great barking breaks forth and two dogs streak out. One is a Jack Russell called Zoe (it is amazing how many of the world's dog breeds originated in Britain). The other is an ugly black mastiff with a mad gleam in her eye and a very well-developed set of teeth. She answers to the name of Lassie. Lassie jinks backwards and forwards at hand-height, barking, growling and slavering. She is decidedly scary. Contrary to appearances, she does not bite.

Alerted by the din, René and Therese will appear. René has just turned sixty. He has keen, intelligent eyes, from which radiate a network of laughter lines. He is possessed of an infectious smile and a gentle sense of humour. He is something big in the town council, the band, the agricultural committee, the local insurance company, the old soldiers from the Algerian War, and heaven knows what else. Everybody likes him.

Therese is popular as well, and busy. Twice a day, summer and winter, come rain or shine, she rounds up the cows from the fields (like most French farms, the land is not in a single parcel) and drives them up the road to the milking parlour, which is on the end of the house. If they are lucky, Alice and David get to help with the driving, for the cows are quite keen to get onto our lawn. If she is very lucky, Alice might get to 'help' with the milking itself. Then we have our milk warm from the cow.

Therese generally has a sweet for the children. When she is not in the milking parlour, we leave the aluminium milk can - the 'pot au lait' - on a log for her. She is generous with her measure. We get our eggs, cider and wood from the farm, too. Vital supplies.

The farm has been in René's family from time immemorial. You can tell that the place is old by the fact that the road swings round it. It was there first. Perhaps part of it once served as a chapel for the community. One winter's night, René pointed out to me a carving of an altar-cup cut into the stone lintel of what was once a door (but which is now blocked up). The carving is so ancient that it can only now be seen by the oblique rays of the outside light. Inside the house there is the kind of arched niche that one sometimes sees in the walls of churches.

The house has all modern amenities but also has a permanent, ageless, feel. Partly this is because of the solidity of the building itself, with its massive construction, stone floors, beams and monumental fireplace. Partly it is to do with that indefinable quality, 'character'.

René has two tractors. One is a thirty-year-old Deutz (German) that looks like a Massey Ferguson: red, sturdy and easy to work on. It lacks a canopy or any such modern frivolities. On one of the wheel arches is fixed a wooden box in which the Jack Russell, Zoe, sits as he (René) drives to his fields. This tractor will probably last forever.

René's other tractor is a Lamborghini. It is only ten years old but it is, says René, 'pas serieuse'. It is too flashy and flimsy. Once, a wheel fell off it. What can one expect? The damn thing hasn't got a goupier (I haven't been able to pin down exactly what a goupier is, but any self-respecting tractor should certainly have one).

Next to the tractor is the zinc tank used to take water out to the beasts in the fields. It is like a large boiler laid on its side and mounted on wheels. Every farmer round here has one of these. They are necessary because so many farms consist of a mass of separate parcels of land. This, in turn, is due to the French inheritance law, the Code Napoleon, a product of the French Revolution.

The French Revolution swept away an enormous amount of what had gone before. Out went all the weights and measures that the Romans had so laboriously spread round their empire two thousand years earlier. Away with livre, sou and denier (pound, shilling and pence), in with franc and centime. Ditch the livre and once (pound and ounce), bring in grammes. Abolish yard, pied and pouce (yard, foot and inch), introduce metres and centimetres.

The French, nostalgic as ever, hold on to some of the old measures even now. Fruit and vegetables are still sold by the pound and there is the pain de livre (pound loaf). Nor do they despise measuring bicycle frames in inches. Mortgage companies are still sometimes referred to as 'preteurs de deniers' (penny lenders) on legal documents.

The revolutionaries would do anything to be different. Whereas traffic used to go on the left, henceforth it would go on the right. They did some other odd things too. They renamed all the days of the week, 'First', 'Second', 'Third' and so on; and called the months 'Rainy', 'Sunny', 'Foggy' (particularly suitable for Normandy) and such like. They even renamed the years. As the Revolution was the start of a new age in world history, 1793 became Year One. They only narrowly avoided creating the hundred-second minute, the hundred-minute hour and the ten-hour day.

Many of these changes were later swept aside. However, the Code Napoleon remains.

The Code Napoleon states that property must be passed down to all children in equal parts. Over the decades, this has caused farms to be split-up, reshuffled and dealt out as randomly as a pack of cards. As a consequence French farmers must spend a disproportionate amount of time (and money) driving from place to place with feed, water and so on - which is why one is so often stuck behind a tractor on French roads.

A little way from René's house is his woodshed. Having reversed his tractor and trailer through a tiny gap between a tree-stump and a wall, and around the corner to the woodshed, René asked me what I thought of his driving. "Superb," I commented. The Normans take pride in understatement in exactly the same way as Yorkshire folk. René shook his head at my extravagance of phrase: "In Normandy we don't say 'superb', we say 'not bad.'" Happen, René lad, happen.

Next door to René's woodpile is his cider store. He has three one thousand litre oak barrels in his store, two of which are over a century old. Near the woodshed, a Renault van rusts quietly to itself among the docks and nettles. A pile of sea shells, put down for the poultry, suggests that René has, like many another Norman, a second house by the sea.

In the stackyard, in front of the milking parlour, is the midden. As winter lengthens, the midden gets higher and higher, strutted and scratched over by the cock of the heap and giving off a good rich smell.

Towards the end of March the heap is moved. It is, as

usual, a communal effort. Albert, René, Desiré and Michel pool their resources for the day to move the muck heap. The four men roll up their sleeves and shovel it, until by late morning the trailer is filled to the board-tops with steaming dung. They take a break for a Norman lunch. Afterwards, the tractor goes off to the far-flung fields. On the main road it will join many others on the same errand.

One Wednesday (in much of France there is no school on Wednesday) René invited the children and me to accompany him to the market at Gavray to sell a calf. On the way he told me about his farm management methods. He does not battery-farm his pigs or his chickens. He feeds his (twenty or so) cows no concentrates and puts up with twenty litres of milk daily from each cow. With concentrates, he could get forty. The only thing he puts on his land is manure.

René is not some fashionable farmer growing organic food at fancy prices. He is doing exactly what his father did, and his father before him. He knows full well that he could force his land to grow more - but he is of the opinion that life is not only a matter of money, that he has a responsibility to his land and his animals.

René is a typical Norman farmer. He does not squeeze the land. He gets low yields. He is uncompetitive. Thousands like him have already been forced out of business.

Gavray market, a traditional affair which takes place each Wednesday, shows the small farmer at work. Most of the livestock are calves and cows.

The parking is confused in a way that is typically French. Some people have parked across two bays, others have stopped in the middle of the road to shake hands, kiss and have a chin-wag. Eventually René manages to slew car and trailer into a space. It looks as though it will take a very long time to sort out the mess at going-home time. And of course it will.

The heart of the market is a long, low, open-sided building, along which run three rows of hitching rails for the beasts. By ten in the morning there are perhaps two hundred farmers and smallholders in the building, mostly with a single animal. You have to be careful where you put your feet. The buyers are instantly recognisable by their black coats. They pass among the farmers and smallholders, looking for likely calves.

I walk through the market, talking to the farmers.

"English?" asks an old man in a shapeless black beret on the edge of the crowd. Yes.

"I thought so. I like the English." Having thus established his credentials, he lowers his voice and continues, "What do you English (I have yet to hear the French call the British anything other than English or Anglo-Saxons) think of us French farmers?" There is a wicked twinkle in his old eye. Is he an agent provocateur?

I look at the scrum of French farmers that stretches as far as the eye can see. "Be honest!" urges the old chap. I look around again. Nobody seems to be taking any notice. I do as I am bid and answer the question as honestly (and as quietly) as I can.

French farmers? They block the autoroutes and disrupt holiday makers. On one occasion they had burnt British lamb. They were regarded in England as selfish so-and-so's who took up cudgels at the first sign of competition, aided and abetted by the most protectionist government in Europe. Such was the 'English' view. What did French farmers think of themselves?

I was very interested to hear what the old man would say - I wanted to know whether that popular devil of the British press, the French farmer, really did have two horns and a tail: besides, it was a subject that might well come up in my exams.

The farmer laughed. "You're as blunt as a Norman." Then he shook his head. "What do we think? We think differently. We think that we are facing oblivion. Our numbers have fallen by two-thirds in forty years, while the number of administrators has trebled. That, malheuresement, is France;

a country where bureaucracy is the only growth industry."

I pointed out that the French farmer was not alone in his troubles. British agricultural workers, too, had been forced off the land in their thousands.

"But Monsieur," my farmer countered, "our countries are very different. We both have the same population but France is three times larger than England (he still meant Britain). When your farm workers left the villages, their houses were bought by people working in the towns. Here, farming is the countryside. There is nothing else. When our 'agriculteurs' go, their houses remain empty, unless we can sell them to the English. The young flee to the towns, the shops and the schools close, and the villages die. Only the old are left. The land empties. We call it 'Le Desert Francais' - the French Desert."

He smiled. "I know you English think of us as bloody-minded law-breakers who are backed-up to the hilt by Paris. Pas vrai. Paris pays lip service to us. In reality the government has no choice but to come into line with Europe. They hope we'll just die quietly."

I looked behind me surreptitiously. Nobody was listening. "But why do you have to take your anger out on British lamb? Aren't we all European now?"

He shook his head emphatically. "If you wish to understand France, you must know that she is not one country, but two. That is a fact that it is always difficult to explain to the English. First we have the cities. You could say they are European; they see their future with the other cities, and they are like them. The crime rate in Paris is probably no different than it is in London, it may be worse for all I know. We, the peasants, are the second France. We don't think of ourselves as Europeans. Why should we? What are we to expect from Europe but the same destruction that your own peasantry has suffered? We are looking down the barrel of a gun - as England did in 1940."

We moved backwards as a large cattle wagon drove in. The children were playing marbles in the dust. There would be the devil to pay when I got them home, but at least they were not bothering me for five minutes.

"Selfish are we?" said the old farmer in mock anger. "Of course we are selfish. Why not? If we don't look after our own interests, who will? Not the government, they're embarrassed by us."

He shrugged. "Eh voila. The politicians say there must be sacrifices for Europe. Our countryside will be one. Our farms will become bigger. We will rip out the hedgerows and drench the land with chemicals and learn to worship the gods of speed and efficiency. It will be the end of a way of life that has lasted for perhaps half a thousand years. It is a life of hard work mostly and it is not rich in possessions. But it is a predictable and orderly life, and to be contented, those are important things. What will we get in its place? Instead of ten poor farmers we shall have one rich one, eight beggars and a thief."

He fished a watch from a side pocket. "Things change but they never get better." I have heard much the same sentiment in Norfolk. Farmers are fatalists the world over. He smiled at me, his blue eyes as clear as a child's, and raised an eyebrow in an expression of - what? Irony? Reflection?

"As for your lamb, Monsieur, you must realise that the French farmer is fighting for his very existence and he is losing his fight. Droves have lost their homes and livelihoods. To do what? They know no other life. In times of crisis it is hotheads more often than saints who take control. Weigh our plight against the damage we do ...and recognise too our virtues. The land you see is as it is because of the small farmer, not the Tourist Board. If you like its tranquillity, its beauty and its lack of crime, do not think too harshly of us. It will be too late to remember our virtues after you have buried us ...and now it is the eleventh hour"

He started to move away. His last remark had not been a profound observation on the fate of the French farmer, he was merely telling me the time - for the cattle market at Gavray hinges around the hour of eleven. I went to gather up the children to watch the proceedings.

There is no auctioneer at Gavray; the bargaining is directly between buyer and seller. There is, however, a referee who tries to make sure that the two parties do not do business before eleven. Any bargaining detected before that hour results in a 250 franc fine for buyer and seller alike. One would think that the referee's job would be impossible in the melee - and so it would if the farmers and buyers themselves did not respect the 'no bargaining before eleven' rule. It is simply not done.

At five minutes to eleven the buyers leave the covered market and form up behind a line painted on the ground, at a distance of perhaps twenty yards. At eleven sharp the referee blows his whistle. They're off! The black-coated mass surges forward and the fleetest take the lead, sprinting across to the shed and the beast that has taken their fancy. First come, first served. Those are the rules.

I watch René with interest. An unusually tall man approaches him and makes an offer. My farmer refuses. The man ups his offer. Again René refuses. The man walks away. After hesitating for a moment, René pushes his way after him through the crowd. He nearly doesn't get his man as the mass suddenly eddies between them, but at last he reaches him. Hands are struck. A ticket changes hands. The deal is done.

René, in fine humour, slaps me on the shoulder. "I had luck there. The rule is that if you turn down an offer and the buyer walks away, you must catch him before he gets too far. Otherwise the offer lapses. He'd nearly gone too far."

"How far is too far?"

René shrugs. "One knows."

We mooch around the market stalls. Everything the discerning farmer could need is here; bundles of ropes of all thicknesses, chains (whole or cut to length), insulators for barbed wire, barbed wire itself, tractor batteries and tyres. Wood saws, milking machines, sapling apple trees ready for the planting, yokes, milking stools. There is a fish van (there always is in a Norman market) with piles of shellfish and live crabs fresh from the sea.

A man cooks sausages and pork chops over a charcoal fire. I share a chop (in bread) with David. Then we go off with René to deliver the calf. The tall buyer is a dealer from Brittany, owner of one of a number of big cattle wagons. The crowd is thick around the wagons.

"Shall I take the calf while you look for the dealer?" René nods his thanks and forces his way through the crowd. I am left holding the animal, which, after first trying to suckle my coat, stands on my foot.

"I say old chap," I mutter. But he ignores me. He may be only a few weeks old, but he can still recognise a greenhorn. I take a census of headgear while I wait for René. Cloth caps outnumber berets by far. René comes back. We deliver the beast. Now he goes to see whether there are any lambs worth buying. Diplomatically, Alice, David and I make ourselves scarce during the business.

We go to see the pigs. Piglets really, varying from babies to three sleek hedonists a yard long who are stretched deliciously against each other in the straw in the back of a farmer's van. The farmer pokes them apart to show to interested parties, accompanied by furious gruntings.

A middle-aged lady, a farmer's wife, stands beside another trailer.

"Can the children look at the pigs?"

"Of course, Monsieur: would they like to stroke them?"

I grin at her. "Will you swap one for my son?"

She eyes David critically. "Non, Monsieur. He'd cost too much to fatten up."

She has a good eye.

The pigs have been transported in various ways. Some are in the back of cars whose rear seats have been taken out, some are in vans, and some in trailers. Many of the wooden trailers are hand-made and donkey's years old, the wood expertly curved to allow for a neck - made to the shape of the animal. (Most of the new trailers are just oblong sheets of aluminium.)

We return to René. In his trailer now are a sheep and her

two lambs. Yes, of course the children can get in to stroke them. He lets down the tailgate. Then he spots a friend and wanders off for a moment to exchange news. Suddenly the sheep make a dash for it. I lunge for the mother and grab her halter. But one of the lambs is out, running between the wheels of the cars.

"René! René!" Frantically I shout for the farmer. Calmly he walks the mother out of the trailer, and the lamb returns to her.

David looks at me pityingly. "René knows what he's doing."

Happen the lad is right.

MILKING TIME

Unimproved country. Doctor Marais.
The battle of Mont Castre. Of tripe and trotters.
What the agent should know.
The Fosse Philosopher.

Within the last fifty years the landscape of Britain has undergone radical change. Hedges have been ripped out, fens drained, woodland chopped down, ponds filled in, meadows ploughed up, chemicals sprayed and monocultures created. The flora and fauna of our country have been subjected to a massive assault. The weapons were bulldozers and DDT, and too often the shock-troops' mindless song was, "You can't stop progress."

Progress, of course, can be halted. The government did it by stepping on the brake instead of the accelerator. It cut 'improvement' grants. Now it has gone into reverse, paying farmers not to grow crops and giving them grants to plant hedges and encourage wildlife.

For those who are saddened by what 'progress' has done to large swathes of our country, the landscape of childhood can be revisited in Normandy. French Departement or not,

LIKE ENGLAND WHEN I WAS A CHILD.

Normandy has the feel of an English county where time has stopped. Traditional farming methods, falling population and a drift to the towns have left it is as England was, a peaceful land of lanes and woods and fields and flowers.

Thick hedges grow on top of steep flower-covered banks. Ancient stone houses sleep in secret valleys, chickens in the yard, beat-up tractor in the barn, cows in the orchard. Hens and geese wander unconcernedly along country roads. The buzzards, barn owls and kestrels still have somewhere to live and something to live on.

The pressure is not on. The field next door is not about to be redeveloped to make a new supermarket. Nor will that hay-strewn barn with its great cider press and century-old oaken barrels become a select development of executive residences. It is a quiet land with many fine beaches which are all but deserted even in high summer. And it is a land that scarcely changes. A map printed in 1947 (to show the major campaigns of the War) can still be used because virtually everything is just the same as it was then.

One can park a car freely - and free of charge, without the feeling that every inch of space has been chopped up, allocated and accounted for, and must return a profit of X pounds per metre per annum.

One of the first things I did upon arriving in Normandy was to put an advert in the local paper to find someone to help me with my written French. In this manner I became friendly with Doctor Marais. The doctor lives in the Carentan Marshes, a low lying fenland which cuts the base of the Cherbourg Peninsula. He is retired and passionate about history.

"History tells all. It lays bare all of man's glory, and all of his evil. If we profit from it, we can turn folly into wisdom. No king ever had a gift so precious. But the past is not safely dead, it is alive and it is powerful. It lives in our languages, our beliefs, our tastes, our cultures and our prejudices. When we care - or dare - to learn from it, it is our greatest servant. When we ignore or deny it, we become its slaves."

Knowing of his interest in history, I mentioned to the doctor that the one thing that English buyers of Norman property seemed to have in common was that they all agreed that Normandy was "like England when I was a child".

"That, Monsieur Biggins," he told me with his characteristic smile, "is because for many thousands of years Normandy and England were not only similar, they were one and the same. Europe was not always as it is now. In the earliest days, swamps, marshes and thick forest covered it, and wolf, bear and boar roamed the continent. The interior was trackless jungle, so man stayed near the coast."

The doctor poked a finger in the air to emphasise his point. "The south of what is now England was more closely linked with our semi-island than it was with the rest of Britain. Wait a moment." He rifled amongst the books which cluttered every surface in his study, coming up in triumph with a red and black volume. It was the 'Histoire de la Normandie'.

"Voila. Ecoutez." He had reached a well-thumbed page. "Normandy was part of the same world as Wiltshire, where arose the mysterious stones of Stonehenge. On both sides of a sea that had never been a frontier, two peoples of the same blood made vows to the sun which they worshipped each year on the sacred day of the summer solstice."

He put the book aside. "But our links do not stop there. The Celts who displaced the builders of the stone circles also lived on both sides of the Channel... they are a people about whom it is easy to become confused. Although they called themselves Celts, the Romans called them Gauls: a name which stuck. We French still call Wales 'Le Pays de Galles', 'the land of the Gauls', and I believe that the Celts of Britain call their language Gaelic."

The doctor's keen eyes met mine.

"The Celts were artists of great vigour who decorated their shields, armour and chariots with powerful and beautiful designs. They were not, however, exactly savoury people. According to ancient sources" - he was rifling through the book piles again - "their nobles let their moustaches grow so long that they hid their mouths and got tangled in their food when they ate. They used amazing colours, brightly dyed shirts with flowing patterns and trousers called breeches."

The doctor's description conjured up an image of a Sixties' Party. He gave up his search for the book and spoke from memory: "They were also said to cut off the heads of their enemies, preserving the most important in boxes and nailing the others to the gates of their camps. According to the Romans they were not above a little cannibalism.

"A red haired, quick tempered people who were both brave and quarrelsome, they loved nothing better than to fight and boast of their conquests. Their religion was bloody and sacrificial. Visitors from other lands wrote of mass human sacrifices in the depths of the oak woods. Mistletoe, flowering in mid winter, was holy to them. Its association with the new year and fertility still survives in your quaint English custom of kissing under it."

The doctor pointed out of the window. The mist had begun to settle in from the marshes. On the far edge of the garden stood a bare tree. A huge dark ball hung in its upper branches. "See, mistletoe. In winter the trees of Normandy drip with the stuff." (It was something I had noticed before. Mistletoe is a parasite and the police can order that it be removed from affected trees. They rarely do but René had told me of a particularly officious local copper who had earned the nickname 'Monsieur Mistletoe' because of the zealousness with which he reached for his notebook whenever he saw the stuff.)

"You understand, Monsieur Biggins, that the Celts had the very latest in technology. Iron. With it they conquered much of Europe, even plundering Rome, at that time a small city-state. As Rome expanded it took its revenge. The Gauls resisted the Romans fiercely, especially here in the Carentan Marshes. Three legions faced them but the marshes, with their few and secret paths, were ideal guerilla country. The defenders made the best of the fens, appearing, striking, disappearing. The Eagles were stopped dead."

A pile of papers overtoppled from a chair. Doctor Marais scooped them up and put them on the table. "It can't have been a very popular posting with the Romans, this trackless bog with its red-haired savages who lured patrols deep into the marsh and then cut them down. And there was the ague, the marsh malaria which makes men shiver and chatter uncontrollably, and the fogs and the cold that seep into the bones. What a country! What a way to fight a war! For months and years the Romans chased the will-o-the-wisps."

Madame Marais appeared with two cups of coffee. Hardly drawing breath to drink, her husband continued.

"Finally the Gaulish chieftain Virodorix - the original of Asterix - rallied his brother tribes for a showdown with the Romans. But Celtic bravery was not matched by discipline. They were just as willing to fight among themselves as against the invaders. Nor were they any match for the Romans in a set-piece battle. Their all-out attack on the Roman camp at Mont Castre failed. The Celtic confederation was utterly defeated. And that," he continued triumphantly, "is when British history began."

He noted my surprise with relish. "Yes, Monsieur. The defeat signalled the end of Celtic resistance on the continent and the Romans followed it up by forcing their captives to provide ships and pilots for the fleet which invaded Britain. The Britons could not resist the legions. The Kentish tribes became tributaries of Rome, and the first recorded British name, Cassivelaunus, entered into history. A thousand years before William, the future of Britain was decided on a hill in Normandy: Mont Castre."

Mont Castre is not far from the doctor's home and he was easily persuaded that we should visit it. He hadn't been there for years, and I was a little dubious of his directions as we left the main road. I don't think he was too sure either. He brightened visibly when he managed to decipher the words 'vieux chateau' on an ancient signpost. We must have made a mistake at the next couple of junctions, for we soon found ourselves back where we had started. Luckily an old lady at the gate of a nearby cottage put us right.

We climbed steadily and finally came to a grassy slope with space for perhaps half a dozen cars. Above us rose a steep slope leading onto a large and heavily wooded hill. Behind us, the hill fell away to the plain.

Doctor Marais pointed to some cliffs in the middle distance: "That, I suppose, is where the Romans had their camp. Come." He guided me up a path through bracken and boulders to a ruined tower, so choked with ivy that from the rear it could hardly be recognised as a building. Below us the plain stretched for miles. The doctor indicated the building. "It is a Roman lookout tower. The Germans used the site for the same purpose in 1944."

We slowly worked our way back down the hill. An old man was scything among some gravestones outside a roofless ruin. Doctor Marais asked him whether he knew the history of the place.

"Pas beaucoup. They say there was a battle here once ...and the roofless building was once a church." He smiled and bent again to his work.

The paths of Britain and France have diverged somewhat since the days of the Celts. There are no longer two Britains, the town and the country. But there are, as the farmer at Gavray market told me, still two distinct divisions in France.

Some rural habits are no longer to the taste of the British (or to French town dwellers for that matter). Norman cooking is not 'nouvelle' it is old. Country people can't afford to be squeamish. They don't get their chickens from Sainsburys, they wring their necks. They say that you can eat every bit of a pig except its grunt. Certainly in Normandy you can see their heads and trotters in butchers' windows, as well as the bits that 'we' eat. I have seen "chicken gizzard salad" on a Norman menu - in English. I think it may have lost something in the translation; that something being its customers.

Then there is tripe. Normandy has many butchers who

claim to sell 'les meilleures tripes du monde' (the best tripes in the world) and 'gold medal tripes'. I confess that I can't understand how one tripe can differ greatly from another - unprocessed raw cow's stomach would, one think, come in few grades. My childhood memory of the stuff is of a white slippery substance as convoluted as a brain and with the unpleasant propensity to slither down the throat.

The first time I tried the Norman variety it was in error; in the form of andouille - tripe sausage. Far from carrying a prominent warning that "these sausages are made from tripe", andouille is a regional delicacy. It was only the consistency that told me what it was. In England tripe is served with onions (to give it some taste), in Normandy it comes in a sort of stew, highly spiced, with carrots and potatoes: 'Tripe a la mode de Caen'. It is delicious.

Even if he has no desire to revive old tastes, the British buyer of a Norman house must relearn old skills. Often it's not simply a matter of switching on the gas boiler to warm the house; you have to go out to the woodshed, spit on your hands, chop sticks and saw logs, then get to work with sticks and paper and (if you are as incompetent at the task as I) with bellows.

While agreeing with his customers that Normandy is "just like England when I was a child", the competent agent will make sure that his customer realises that there are important practical differences.

For example, metered water, although an excellent conservation measure, can work out to be very, very, costly if a pipe bursts and the leak goes undiscovered for a long time. And in some country districts (ours included) you don't put the rubbish out for the dustman, you take it to the tip yourself.

Again, it is the law in France that chimneys must be swept each year. If a valid sweep's certificate cannot be produced, then fire insurance is invalid. This is complicated by the fact that getting a sweep to come when he says he will is difficult in the French countryside. (A sub-plot of one of Hergé's 'Tintin' books is Captain Haddock's repeated attempts to get a broken stair mended. The mason gives a bewildering array of excuses as he fails to keep appointment after appointment. Hergé was drawing from life. In rural France, appointments are regarded as declarations of intent rather than binding agreements.)

The agent should also be able to advise on French electricity. This means knowing its cost structure for varying supply, that ring-mains are illegal, the different tariffs that can be had, and that it is impossible to run a British electric cooker from the French three-phase power supply. If he's worth his salt, he will know the difference between SECAM and PAL (not a dog food), the difference between French and British plumbing and roofing, and a thousand other things beside.

It's a fair assumption on the buyer's part that the agent will know this kind of stuff. The agency charges are three or four times higher than they are in Britain, so the buyer expects 'cost plus' to be equalled by 'service plus'. Also the agent is often the only person in the transaction who can speak both English and French.

Sadly, it would appear that I am not the only agent who has been told to 'learn on the job'. Others have begun their careers as I did, as ignorant of French laws as the customers they serve but without, alas, the helping hand of a Peter Edwards. The mistakes by which such agents learn usually concern boundaries, access and services. An amusing example of the latter was given to me by Mr Verger, the fosse septique man.

The fosse septique (septic tank) is an institution in France (there are three million of them). Not only is it a system of sewage, it is also a living organism which must be treated with respect. This is a lesson that many owners of holiday homes who have brought disinfectant from Britain have learned to their cost. After cleaning their toilets a few times, they wonder why there is a nasty smell. The answer is simple. Their fosse is stone 'mort'. Micro organisms do not thrive on ammonia.

The fosse must be cosseted. Like many of us, it prefers its native food; the specially prepared toilet cleaners available for it. In fact, not only must toilets be cleaned with specially formulated cleaners, the FS is partial to supplementary feeding. Products are available to double its life-span, though the more frugal simply feed it on yeast.

Mr Verger is an expert on the FS He puts them in for a living. The first time that I saw him he was digging a hole and some trenches outside an empty and almost ruinous house, in an area where I had several properties. I thought that it would be useful to know a man who could do such a job and returned on the following day to talk to him. I timed my arrival for twelve o'clock, when, as I had anticipated, he was just on the point of knocking off for lunch. The sky was darkening ominously.

Mr F. is a small man with bristling black hair and a ferocious look. "Nice day" was my opening gambit. (The French discuss the weather just as much as the English, and often in the same ironical terms.)

"Mouron weather" he grunted.

"Mouron weather?" I repeated blankly.

"That's right. There's been so much rain lately, it's flushing them out of their holes."

"What's a mouron?" I asked.

He looked at me in surprise. "Small creature, like a lizard. Black, with bright yellow markings. They live in dry, dark places. In old houses they lurk behind the back-plate of the fire; outdoors, under tree roots. Heavy rain always flushes them out." He shuddered. "Nasty creatures."

I was still none the wiser.

"Well then" said Mr Verger, thawing a little "let's see if we can't find one for you. You may have luck." He led me to the front of the building, where a concrete plate was let into the ground. He lifted it: "This is the kind of place they like."

I peered down into the ground. The hole was about nine inches deep. In it was the stopcock for the water supply.

"See anything?"

"A toad... wait a minute, there is something else." I reached into the ground and hooked out an animal; it was, as Monsieur Verger had said, like a lizard. It made no complaint but lay docile on my hand, blinking stupidly in the livid pre-storm light. I looked into the trap again. There was a second animal. This, too, I fished out. It lay as unmoving as its mate. They were, as Mr Verger had said, the most brilliant black and yellow.

"I wouldn't do that" counselled Mr Verger with a short laugh. "They're poisonous."

Hastily I put the creatures back and replaced the cover. 'Mouron', as I found out later, is the Norman dialect word for a salamander.

Monsieur Verger invited me to join him while he ate. The heavens opened as we entered the building. Two years of drought were being followed by two years of rain.

We sat on a granite cider press, the only furnishing the room possessed, and Mr F. offered me a cigarette and some cider. I declined the cigarette, but the cider was good. Yes, he agreed, he was indeed excavating a hole and channels for a fosse septique. He cut several slices from a large sausage, fished out a small jar of pickled gherkins, and began his lunch.

The rain began to fall, making a din on the corrugated iron roof. A cow lowed mournfully in the next room. I asked Mr F. if he had a pump for emptying septic tanks? "Bien sur Monsieur."

In that case I had a story which would while away the time while he ate. It was a tale told me by a friend in England, a one-time farm worker. Farmers are notoriously 'careful', and my friend's ex-boss was no exception. He had 'done up' a cottage on his farm and let it out very successfully. The holiday home used a septic tank for its drainage and when it was unmistakeably full the farmer decided to empty it himself. Consequently he hired a drainage tank and pump.

It seemed easy enough. Simply remove the septic tank's cover, drop in the pipe and turn on the pump. The first two parts of the operation had, indeed, gone to plan. Then the farmer switched on the suction pump. He had, however, overlooked one small detail. The pump was designed to blow as well as to suck. The farmer had turned the switch the wrong way. Instead of being drawn from the septic tank into the waiting receptacle, the effluent was blown back at high pressure into the holiday home, with, as they used to say of the 'Carry On' films, hilarious consequences: or so my friend the farm worker thought, though the farmer didn't agree.

Monsieur Verger seemed to find the story amusing. He gagged on his cider and sausage, and I had to hammer his back hard. The cow mooed in protest.

The Frenchman now proceeded to cap the tale. His story also concerned an Englishman, a septic tank, and a holiday home. Well, not a home exactly. It was a big old barn on the side of a hill, which the Englishman had purchased through an agent, another 'anglais'.

Mr F. came onto the scene when the buyer wanted a quote for a fosse septique. One look at the place had been enough to tell him that it was totally out of the question. There was a good half an acre of land (I translate from Mr Verger's hectares) but it was all uphill. One can't run sewage uphill and the underlying stone, being granite, was impossible to excavate.

Then and there the buyer and the agent had had a furious altercation, of which Mr Verger had not, of course, understood a word. He tapped me on the knee:

"I may not speak anglais, mais, evidement, there was a story there. Like you, Monsieur, I am partial to a good story." He wiped his mouth with the back of his hand and deliberately lit a cigarette. "I tracked down the original owner to the next village. He told me that originally he had offered nearer an acre of land, half of it downhill. And the price he had asked had been 'correct'. The agent, however, was very overbearing. He proceeded to beat the owner down in front of the English client. He offered thirty thousand francs less than the asking price. The owner needed the money, and he sold."

Mr Verger took another pull of cider.

"When the time came to sign the sale's agreement, the owner came up with a provision; the lower half of the land was not to be included in the sale. That didn't upset either the buyer or the agent. As you know, Monsieur, land is not worth much around here, and besides, half an acre was quite enough as far as the buyer was concerned. The agent, however, insisted that the owner pay the Geometre's fees to readjust the boundaries. The owner put up a show of reluctance, then agreed. The land was divided and the sale went through."

"And when the new owner tried to get permission to change the usage of the building from agricultural to residential, it was refused because there was no room for a fosse septique?" I remembered Peter Edwards' training.

Mr Verger laughed immoderately once more. The rain beat harder outside. Finally he came back to his story:

"Voila, Monsieur. The purchaser had to buy the other half acre. Of course the price was a little higher than the agricultural rate. Sixty thousand francs."

He raised a finger. "But, 'attention', Monsieur, the original owner was only an ignorant countryman: a peasant like myself. It was not the fact that he had been out-bargained that made him plot his revenge. It was the way in which it had been done. Arrogance is a dangerous failing. When it is coupled with ignorance, it can be fatal."

It sounded as though Monsieur Verger was a philosopher. Maybe he had learned to be one. In France there is a university qualification in refuse collection and doubtless another in waste disposal. To get into higher education for these (or any other) courses the student must study several 'core' subjects, of which philosophy is one. So Mr Verger may well have spent several years pondering on the enigma of man's higher nature in order to become qualified to dig holes to cater for his baser one. In any event a degree of - or preferably A Degree In - philosophy is very useful when living in rural France.

Ignorance and arrogance are a fatal mixture?

"In England," I replied, "we say that where there's muck

there's money."

There is no equivalent saying in French, and the thought tickled Mr Verger.

"In your industry, Monsieur," he retorted as he carefully wiped the blade of his knife and folded it back into the shaft, preparatory to returning to his work, "the reverse would also appear to be the case."

PONT DE SOULEUVRE

A scythe a snake and a son. Walls and woodpiles.
A walk. In search of the Bee Jay.

"Snake!"

Our orchard has precisely one hundred apple trees, ninety-four of which are for cider. I keep the path around it cut with a Father Time scythe that I discovered in a barn and bought for a hundred francs. With the scythe came memories. The farmer told me of the days before the War, when his farmhouse had been full of labourers and men would scythe the fields ten abreast. No joking. No chat. Hard, exhausting work; a young man's game.

He even gave me a demonstration. Hip movement is important in scything, as is keeping the blade good and sharp. For this, I was told, you must always have on your belt a whetstone and a cowhorn full of cider to keep it oiled. The cowhorn should be stoppered with a leaf. Naturally you must also have plenty of cider to keep the reaper oiled.

I can vouch for the fact that it is hard work.

It was a Sunday in high summer when David came running down the path in a state of great excitement, shouting, "Snake!"

As my son is quite capable of swearing black is white, it

was a somewhat sceptical trio who followed him into the jungle. Sure enough, he was right; a snake was sunning itself in the middle of the path. It was a beauty, two or three feet long, and it quickly made itself scarce. There was great excitement. The orchard was placed out of bounds. Books were consulted. René was questioned. It was a grass snake and quite harmless.

René was not surprised: did I want him to get rid of the thing? The previous year he had destroyed a nest of 'viperes' on our property. He shivered at the thought. No, he did not like grass snakes, harmless or not. They milk the cows at night.

How a snake can milk a cow is beyond me. There would seem to be a couple of practical difficulties. For one thing, I don't think cows lie down to sleep. Whenever I camp near the beasts they seem to spend the entire time blundering into my tent, which means that they must be upright. Then, the snake has no arms; so how can it get the milk out? Were it to fix itself on the udder and suck, would it not have problems with its breathing and simply fall off?

Enquiring into the exact nature of how a snake milks a cow is difficult in a foreign language, so the subject has become one of those little jokes that exist at the heart of any family. David is of the opinion that several animals must be involved. According to his theory, the dogs bring out the milking stool, the moles do the milking, and the snake lies under the udders with his mouth open.

There are certainly plenty of moles. We see them scuttling across tracks on damp days. One morning we found three of the gentlemen in velvet dead by the roadside. There was not a mark on them. Could they have succumbed through overworking on the previous night?

There is wildlife all around us. Sometimes it gets too close. Our house is a great old stone pile, how old I have no idea. At some time in the past an attempt has been made to 'gentrify' it; to pretend that it is constructed of finished stone blocks. To do this, the irregular stone frontage has been rendered with cement. Symmetrical white lines have been grooved into the rendering to suggest mortar between blocks. This is a very common feature of old Norman farm houses.

Now the facing is slowly crumbling away, leaving ideal points of ingress for mice, voles and shrews. They pitter-patter in the walls on winter nights. We used to find them every morning in our humane mousetrap. We would release them into the orchard (from which they probably scuttled straight back in).

Had our neighbours known of our humane mousetrap, they would doubtless have been highly amused. Their answer to rodents is the same as it was to the aristocracy: the guillotine.

Guillotine mousetraps can be bought in the single-user version or the multi-user 'chop-em-all special', which consists of three blades in series. These are to be had at the ironmonger's shop, close by the bridge in Villedieu. This shop is much as an ironmonger must have been in England between the wars. From it can be bought rat-proof meat safes to hang from the ceiling, yokes, milking stools, storm lanterns, besoms and tallow. The smaller purchases are wrapped in twenty-year-old newspapers.

The back of our place, which faces north, was such a mouse-run that I had it entirely re-rendered. Now it is a forbidding cliff, pierced only by three insignificant little windows (all the others are at the front). There must still be a way in somewhere. Scufflings can yet be heard in the walls after nightfall. Alice finds the scampering behind her headboard comforting. She thinks it is the Russian hamsters.

The hamsters were pressed on me by a very kind French lady whose house I was selling. ("Your children will love them.") They were the most boring animals I have ever come across. They spent the whole day sleeping in their shelter. Only after we had gone to bed would we hear their wheel creaking its way round. Boring or not, they certainly were not dumb. One day when I came to clean out their cage, they had disappeared.

There is space on our plot for other creatures, too. On one boundary of the property is the chicken house, a building divided into two stalls by an internal wall. Each stall is perhaps six feet by four, and high enough to stand in. In front of the chicken house is the run, wired off against foxes (I have smelt foxes in the garden, though I have never seen them). In the run are two rabbit cages. Of course, the Normans do not keep bunny as a friend, but for the pot. We, being born cowards, have kept neither rabbits nor chickens.

Then there are the woodsheds. They say round here that you can tell a man by the size of his woodpile. Mine, I regret to say, is pitifully small. But I do have a lot of wood waiting to be sawn up. I have my suspicions about one of the stacks. Ann tells me that there is a great scuffling in it at night, and there are lots of wisps of grass caught in the logs. Could we have a fouine?

I first heard of the fouine on an August day when we had been invited to tea at the home of some friends. They rent a massive old place with half an acre of land, for which they pay about the same price as it would cost for the smallest flat in England.

In the grounds is a magnificent granite barn pierced by several arches and doors. It serves as the childrens' playhouse. Lloyd and Adam proudly showed us (myself, Alice and David) around. Lloyd, at ten years of age the oldest of the children, led us into the first bay. Here we climbed a wooden ladder to the upper floor, which was piled high with bales of winter feed. As is often the case in Normandy, the floor was made of a mixture of clay and straw, probably a foot thick, laid onto massive oak beams.

At the risk of invoking their mothers' wrath, I helped the children up the pile of bales. Finally we came level with the roof timbers. All the joints were pinned with oak pegs; not a nail was to be seen. The wood was as sound as on the day it had been cut. The carpentry was beautiful, functional and massive. An inspiration. That roof would have graced a

Guild Hall. Decades of spiders' webs festooned the wooden spans in the gloom under the roof tree. It was warm up there.

Suddenly David appeared with a broken hen's egg from the very top of the heap.

"The bats bring them up here," Lloyd told me, pointing up to where a dozen of the creatures hung motionless from the beams.

I explored the rest of the building in the course of a game of hide-and-seek. In the next bay was the farmer's tractor and an old-fashioned horsetrap for Sunday outings. Although I suppose it had lain in its corner for the best part of sixty years, the trap was in excellent condition; even to the canvas roof and sides. It had two iron mounting steps, and its wheels came up to my chest. It must have needed a carthorse to pull it. Alice was hidden inside.

The chickens were in the next bay. Two eggs lay on a pile of straw in an old stone trough. The bats hadn't been there yet. Here I found Adam and David.

A couple of cattle stalls came next, their floors six inches deep in what must have been ten years' accumulation of cow muck. No-one in their right minds would hide in there.

Then, behind an archway choked with nettles, was a room filled with a great mound of logs. Carefully, I climbed the unstable pile and onto the first floor. A long room stretched before me. That's where I caught Lloyd. I lingered to study two mouldering piles of horse tack. There were great collars for carthorses, leather harnesses and metal bits; more than I know the use of or the words for. The remains of a specialised world which once boasted experts on every farm in Europe.

"Come on!" Alice counted to twenty.

The last part of the building was the house. All that remained of the furnishings was an agricultural calendar dated 1986.

The downstairs was a single smoke-blackened room. Its main feature was its Norman fireplace. This was about four feet high and four wide, and framed by three blocks of dressed granite, two uprights and a mantlepiece. The fireback was blackened by great tar globules. A notched iron rod, to take the cooking pot, hung down from the chimney. The hearth was level with the floor, which was made of beaten clay. Above the mantlepiece was a woodwormed and perished rifle rack. A door led onto the stairs.

The upstairs consisted of three small rooms, separated by thin panelling which did not quite reach the ceiling. I heard a noise on the stairs: "Got you!" shouted Alice triumphantly. "Don't have much idea do you? You're it again!" I left the little house, crossing myself instinctively as I passed the disjoncteur.

The sequel to the story came two weeks afterwards, when our friends gave a party to which they invited their landlords. The elderly couple were clearly enjoying the dancing. ("We don't do this kind of thing in France," confided the farmer.)

I taxed him about the bat. He shook his head: "It is not a bat, Monsieur. It is a fouine." A what? Longer than a cat, not as high as a dog, sharp little eyes, close together. They lived in the wood pile. A stoat? A weasel? He shrugged.

At home, I looked up the word. It was a marten - the rarest of the native land mammals of the British Isles: trapped and poisoned to virtual extinction. "Probably in the past the pine marten often lived close to farmyards, as the beech marten still does today in continental Europe."

I questioned René's daughter, Marie-France, about the marten. Oh yes, a perfect nuisance. Worse than foxes. At least foxes eat the chickens; martens just bite off their heads and drink their blood.

I kept the marten in mind during my brother's visit, when he would spend his evenings painting a barn owl that he had found dead on the road. I reminded him to bring the bird indoors at nightfall. If it can't get chicken, I wouldn't put a little owl-napping past the fouine.

At least once a day, Ann and I take the dog, Flavie (daughter of René's dog, Zoe), for a walk. Flavie is a good farm dog who seems easily to have become accustomed to a life of luxury and lying on sofas and beds. But a real dog for all that; a dog that will bury things and dig them up only when they have reached the requisite state of rottenness.

Flavie is a dog that insists on her own social life and who nips off at every opportunity to see her mother on the farm. As a puppy she had to be forcefully discouraged from chasing the locals on their bikes and 'put-puts'. (An old lady whom she chased surprised me by screaming, "I'll kick your teeth down your throat you filthy cur!" I sympathised with her, but it was not the reaction I would have expected from an old lady in England.)

We turn left out of the gate. The road, the width of a tractor, winds down to a stream where we stop a while to watch the animals which we cannot identify. They look like a small coypu; but do coypu exist in Normandy, or are they some species not found in Britain? Sometimes Guillaume, Albert's grandson, can be seen fishing the stream for eels.

The road continues upwards between two faces of crumbling shale; rock so soft that it can be broken by hand, covered with liverworts. If a car should approach, we stop and stare at the driver. This is an occupational hazard in the French countryside and one that used to annoy us when we were on the receiving end. Now we goggle like the locals. We expect to know the occupants.

The hedgerows are several feet above the fields, perched on steep banks that were originally formed when men first went into the great wood and hacked out fields, leaving the decaying trunks around the edges to keep the animals in. This is the Bocage.

The banks are colourful. Yellow primroses light them into March. April brings the orchids in clusters that stretch for mile after mile, even along the sides of the main roads. In May the foxgloves come. There my botanical knowledge ends.

Across the way, fields and hedges rise toward Mont Robin, the second highest point in the Departement (county) of Manche. Mont Robin was used by the Germans during the War to observe the Channel (when it wasn't too foggy). It is topped now by a television transmitter.

To the left is the muddy path, another of our walks. It runs through a hollow which becomes a lake when the weather is wet, which it was throughout 1992. A Norman farmer once told me that "if it rains on St Barnabus's day (in May), it will rain for forty days, but if St Medard wears him out (i.e. it is fine on the 8th of June) it will be dry again." Fairly incomprehensible stuff. Easier to say that if it didn't rain that summer it was a miracle.

He also told me that I must on no account sow carrots on St Medard's day, advice that I took to heart. The French take their carrots seriously. I remember walking past a newsagents' in St Lo, the chief town of The Manche, and noting the headline of Ouest France, the main daily newspaper of Western France, which covers a population of a couple of million. "Carrot crop in danger!" it screamed.

On many occasions I have carried the kids and the dog over the worst of the muddy path, and, once or twice, Ann too. But leave the muddy path for another day. Instead, follow the road for another two hundred yards to enter a hamlet of four or five houses, all of splendid stone, for the Normans excel in building in stone. Some of the houses are roofed in rusting corrugated iron, a sure sign that at one time they were thatched.

Here lives the tanner. Sometimes a goat can be seen in his garden, sometimes a goat skin. Across the road is the chimney sweep's house. Everywhere in the country the people have their own field, some chickens, a few cages of rabbits for the pot, perhaps a sheep or two, their orchard, and, of course, their woodpile. Cows graze under the apple trees. There are more cows and apples to the square whatever-it-is in Normandy than anywhere else in Europe.

The dogs bark madly. They aren't used to walkers (it is regarded as an English eccentricity) and set up a howl as soon as we are within sniffing distance of the hamlet, keeping it up until we are far beyond it. A pair of small dogs race out to see us. One of them is a black Scotch terrier whom we call Jock and who David insists that Flavie will one day marry. They do seem to be very interested in each other.

None of the other dogs get near us, being chained up. I don't know why the French bother with dogs if not for security - and in Normandy there is hardly any crime. It cannot be for companionship, because dogs are not often allowed indoors. The look of horror from a French visitor when she saw our animal sitting on the sofa would have been worth a photograph.

Beyond the hamlet, a track runs up by the side of a trickle of water. By the edge of the track is an ivy-smothered stone trough, round and shadowed, half-filled with clear cold water. This, I should imagine, is perfect whisky water; for we are on the edge of granite country and the water, to compensate for that hard, hard, rock, is soft. Unfortunately the trough seems always to carry a burden of a drowned vole or two, as well as its two resident frogs.

A few yards up the track stands another of those stone barns that litter the land. Inside are a pair of great wooden cartwheels almost as big as a man. A yoke lies against the wall. Outside, abandoned in the grass, are an old horse-drawn plough and roller.

Lichens grow on the trunks of trees and on tired old farm gates. In summer the butterflies are everywhere, flitting in and out in waves of red and black and yellow. If the children are with us, it is difficult to dissuade them from picking up dead wildlife - empty mice, dead sparrows, dehydrated slow-worms, crushed frogs, moles or adders - to bury in their animal cemetery. Bizarre.

Often on our walk we hear a woodpecker furiously hammering away at a tree. It reminds me of one of those children's foli-de-rols you can buy to put in party bags; a little plastic bird mounted on a spring that can be 'boinged' about.

The area is a paradise for birds. A pair of buzzards mew over our house. They nest somewhere over towards Desiré's place. A heron sometimes stands in the field by the stream. Kestrels can often be seen sitting on fences by the roadside. Birds of prey are at the top of the food chain. If there is poison in the land they are the first to go. But there is little poison here. Chemicals are not used, and fish and small game abound. But not rabbits. Perhaps the buzzards get them.

We have seen no less than four brilliant black and yellow salamanders on our walk, flushed out, as Monsieur Verger told me, by the rain. All had been crushed by cars. René tells me that they used regularly to fall into the holes he dug for his fence posts. Red squirrels are common too.

There are badgers as well. A neighbour found one stunned beside the road and put it in the boot of his car along with his dog. By the time the man got home, the badger had recovered sufficiently to bite off the poor dog's testicles.

But the culmination of Norman wildlife is the 'B. J.' (pronounced Bee Jay). To be successful, the naturalist must, of course, be in the right place at the right time. This dedication can occasion considerable discomfort and effort, especially if the species to be observed is rare.

Maps must be annotated, provisions prepared, suitable clothing selected, time set aside, plans made and revised, and transport arranged. Sometimes this preparation and expense are crowned with success, sometimes they are all in vain. The risk is worthwhile for a chance to see the Bee Jay.

As the creature can be categorised as neither animal nor bird, its needs are of a very peculiar and demanding nature. Not only must it have a cliff, but that cliff must be overhanging and at least two hundred feet high. Elsewhere in the world, artificial habitats have had to be constructed for this endangered species, so Normandy is indeed fortunate to provide a natural one.

The beast exists only in a single colony in a remote valley of the river Vire. Here it has taken for its habitat an ancient work of man, the remains of an erstwhile railway bridge, the Pont Souleuvre.

The bridge was designed by no lesser person than Monsieur Eiffel himself. The line across it must have been an impressive sight in its heyday. Running for three hundred yards, it rested on six granite pillars which are built up from the bed of an awesome gorge. It survived, unscathed, five hundred bombing raids during the War, only for the spans, growing dangerous, to be blown up on the order of France's Minster of Transport.

For twenty years the massive pillars stood deserted. Then, one exciting weekend, this perfect habitat was discovered and colonised by the Bee Jay. Now wildlife enthusiasts flock in their thousands to see it.

It might be thought that excessive observation would scare the creatures away. Not a bit of it. Far from being shy, the Bee Jay appears to revel in the limelight.

The discomfort that I mentioned earlier is in approaching their eyrie, which is situated on the third of the stone pillars, two hundred feet above the valley floor. To reach it, one must cross a walkway which has been constructed where the rail-spans once ran. A trifling fee is charged for using it.

The walkway is a flimsy affair and, as seems inevitable with light suspension bridges, there are a number of 'swayers' among those who cross. They throw all their weight first this way, then that, to get a good movement going. The hundred-foot traverses between pillars on this rocking lifeline, with the valley floor far below, are, however, a very small price to be paid to observe the extremities of behaviour of the unusual creature whose lofty habitat this is.

The Bee Jay's plumage is often highly colourful but it is most remarkable for the perfect symbiotic relationship it shares with its human attendants, each being completely dependent on the other for its survival. The attendants are instantly recognisable by their vivid headgear and habit of chewing gum throughout the daylight hours. They prepare the Bee Jay for its flight by encasing the nervous creature in a harness and attaching it to a rope.

The Bee Jay is now escorted - in some case pushed - to the edge of the awful chasm. It makes its exit in a variety of ways; possibly forwards, possibly backwards, possibly dangled head-first over the precipice. Two hundred feet below, a crowd stand at the river edge, waiting for the creature to leap. Ten feet from the Bee Jay, behind a safety barrier but often decidedly nervous for all that, are more spectators.

This is the moment of truth for the Bee Jay. If it utters: "Non, non" - one of the alarm-calls of the species - it is liable to be abused by the crowd, incensed that they may be deprived of their sport.

At this point, the creature faces an awful dilemma. It is difficult to know whether it is braver to jump or to refuse. Most jump, some with the hair-raising screams associated with sacrifice, some in silence.

For several seconds the Bee Jay is in dreadful freefall. Then, apparently only inches above the water, it is arrested. For the novice this is the worst moment of all. Just when all seems to be over, the creature is jerked up almost to the level at which it began. Flapping its arms in a vain attempt to fly out of its dreadful predicament, the beast 'boings' up and down, before finally coming to rest with its head inches above the water. It is then ignominiously fished out and returned to dry land.

As the species counts few females, there can be little hope for the future of the Bungy Jumper.

ANCIENT "BOULANGERIE"

Notaires. Fog. Calvados.
Arthur, Avalon, Britons and Bretons.
The Six Potato Man v. the Willow-pattern Ghost.

Looking for a house in Britain is easy. You simply breeze into a shop, look at what's on the wall and pick out a few details for closer perusal at home.

That is not the way of it in rural France.

Most French country properties are sold by notaires. The notaire is a government appointed official who mixes the duties of a solicitor and an estate agent. He (I have never met a female notaire) is a highly respected figure in the rigidly-hierarchical social structure of the French countryside. He is commonly addressed as 'maitre' (master).

Apart from the fact that small towns do not have estate agents, there are several advantages in buying from a notaire. He is much cheaper than an agent. His fees are regulated by the government and are much lower than agency fees which are set by themselves. The difference can be thousands of pounds.

Then there is conservatism. Many country folk would no

more dream of asking an agent to sell their house than they would of asking a witch doctor to hear their confession. So the rural notaire often has a far better selection of 'character' houses than the agent. This, of course, is precisely the type of property that the English buyer is normally interested in.

But there are drawbacks. The notaire's office often takes a bit of finding. It is (like much of rural France) closed between twelve and two. Then, in order to see his 'black book' of property details it is usually necessary to see the notaire himself. This means making an appointment or waiting, which is fine if one has time to spare, but not much good if one is on holiday and in a rush.

When one finally does get to meet the notaire, he is generally a very pleasant and knowledgeable man. However, he does not speak English (there must be exceptions but I have never met one: the only groups who generally do speak English are doctors and teachers).

The notaire's property details (in French, obviously) vary from the handwritten to those produced on a laser printer. Frequently they are abbreviated: 'toit ard, verg, F4' ('slate roof, orchard, F4'). F4? What the 'F' means I have never discovered, but the '4' refers to the number of main rooms.

As this system is a century or two old, kitchens, WC's and bathrooms do not get included in the count. A house, then, will sometimes be simply described as having four rooms. If further information is given, it never includes room dimensions.

The service of Monsieur le Notaire is, not surprisingly, geared to French expectations, not British ones. To those who are used to a 'self-service' approach and have neither much time nor a good command of French, his 'etude' can be a very confusing and frustrating place. Which is where the British agent, if he is astute, can score heavily.

Given that the notaire usually has a good stock of houses, it is not unusual for that agent to do a deal with him so as to get access to his properties. The agency for which I was working had arranged that I do such a 'mass take on' with a notaire in a country district.

This notaire was exceptional in that he left his books of property details in the reception area for all to see. He had a very nice assistant who dealt with property sales. At first she and I visited the houses together. After a while, she would simply give me a map reference, a quick potted history and, if the place was empty, the keys.

One day I set off to see what she called 'The Old House'. There I was to experience again that feeling, common in Normandy, that the past and the present are very close.

It was a misty day.

One of the two preconceptions that the French have about Britain is, of course, that our cuisine is awful. There is some truth in this. Eating in a French restaurant has everything to do with food and nothing to do with snobbery. However, I feel that such a criticism from a people who have yet to make the culinary quantum leap from tripe to fish and chips is, to say the very least of it, debatable.

The second belief that all Frenchmen hold about England is that ours is a foggy island. Until I got bored with the game, I would make a point of remarking on the fog each time I drove through a Norman pea-souper to take on a house.

The reaction varied. I was either told that fog is very rare (this usually after a white-out had lain over the entire peninsula for at least a week) or that it was much worse than last year (last year was exactly the same). I would then be told that at any rate the fog is much worse in England; it is always foggy in England.

I have lived in England close on forty years, in the north, the south, the east, the Midlands and on the Welsh borders. I have never seen anything like Norman fog. Or at least I have seen nothing so persistent since the yellow smogs that held York in their grip when I was a child, smogs caused by coal smoke which could not escape. That is the England the average Frenchman sees when he closes his eyes; a film of London in an adaptation of a novel by Dickens - swirling fog and gaslights.

In winter Normandy has sea-fogs, low-cloud fogs and marsh fogs: sometimes mixed together. In summer these frightening murks give way to more localised and less persistent vapours. They are tree-mists, the product of thousands of orchards breathing out at night. From Cherbourg to Avranches you dive down into them and up again; one minute in a white-out, the next in brilliant sunshine. In summer the mists normally burn off in the morning. That summer was far from normal and they had persisted.

The Old House had evidently once been a place of some importance. A stone flight of steps led up to the massive front door. I knocked. A face appeared at a window, a slight lady with the rheumy, fearful eyes of the very aged. She disappeared but did not come to the door. I was left kicking my heels.

After a while, the owner arrived. He told me that the old lady was a tenant and was shortly to go into a home. He showed me around. In the grounds was a confused acre of banks and brambles surrounded by a scrub-choked moat. This, I was told, had been the site of a Norman 'chateau'. The Lord of the ancient stronghold had evidently not been popular. The whole place, keep, dungeons and all, had been torn down stone by stone by the peasants during the revolution of 1789.

At a little distance from the broken ground was a roofless circular building made of flint and slate, with thousands of niches let into the inner walls. It was strikingly similar to one I had seen in a museum of rural life in Sussex: the pigeon tower of the chateau.

A great tithe barn, over a hundred and fifty feet long, stood apart, evidence, as was the pigeon tower, of the one-time importance of the place. In the barn were two hay-carts. These were mighty wagons with wheels as high as a man, blood-brothers of the tumbrils used to take the aristocrats to the guillotine. "If you sell the place for me, they are yours, Monsieur" the owner told me, having noted my interest.

He led me onwards, holding up an electric wire with his

handkerchief so that I could duck under it. Our passage left a trail in the wet grass. At some distance from the house stood the boulangerie (bake house), a small building with a massive clay bee-hive oven at one end. These ancient buildings are common in the Norman countryside, always being situated a good way from the main building for safety's sake.

Next to the house was a forge, containing bellows, horse brasses and a curiously slotted wooden frame which the owner explained had been used to make rope. A fairy-tale well with a steep little roof stood beside the forge.

The house itself, built with stones from the chateau, had seen better days. Damp had got in here and there. The beams in the cellar had been eaten by woodworm to a depth of four inches and the wide, dark, wooden staircase had been similarly attacked. I had been wasting my time knocking on the front door. It was held in place by great rusting iron crossbars and can't have been opened for years.

The changes made to the house over the centuries had been largely cosmetic. The electrics were quite literally shocking. An unscreened toilet sat in one corner of a bedroom. What wires and pipes there were, were laid onto, rather than into, the walls. Walking round the place, I sensed the present itself to be but a thin veneer stretched over the past.

I visited the Old House some weeks later to take photographs. The day was sunny, and I could appreciate the scenery as I had not been able to before. The position was quite stunning, on a wide ledge high above a valley. The little fields of the bocage stretched for perhaps two miles to the opposite side of the valley, where thick forest began.

The house was empty now, the old woman carted off. Briefly I made a tour, confirming room dimensions. The place would certainly need a lot of renovation, but the structure was sound enough and the rooms were large and well proportioned.

I love old buildings and would normally have lingered awhile, taking in the atmosphere. Not in that house. Although it was full day, there was an odd 'feel' to the place. Something was wrong, disjointed, there. Wisps, wraiths of the past, 'ghosts', lingered just beyond the edge of vision, neither malignant nor evil but indefinably strange. Not to be touched. Disquietening.

When I returned the key to the notaire's assistant she looked at me quizzically. "Well?" She asked. I looked at her and she gave me a little smile. She knew more about the house than she had told me. What it was, I never found out.

There is something in Normandy itself which seems to lie outside the shackles of time. This came home to me most keenly on a July day in the Year of our Lord, nineteen hundred and ninety-two. The farmers had just finished silage making. Large bags of grass lay in the fields, warming up to produce winter feed for the animals.

It was a special day. Calva day. Only farmers who were farming before 1958 are allowed to make calvados without an excise licence, and they are limited to a mere ten litres per annum. It is made by distilling the remains of the previous year's cider. The job is done by a contractor. I had gone to René's to leave the puppy with him, for Ann and the children were in England and I was taking customers out that day.

The contractor, a fine old gaffer dressed in regulation blue overalls, was seated in René's kitchen and partaking of smoked ham, pickled gherkins and, bien sur, cider. His alembic (still) seemed to belong to the same general family as Stevenson's Rocket. He started the heating process. The boiler was a wood burner - like all fires in Normandy.

Crackling away under the apple trees in the warmth of summer, with the air hazy from the slight fumes of ten thousand distillations, the ancient machine was itself a distillation of all things Norman, past and present.

Calvados is assigned almost magical properties by the older country folk. Just about any wound can be cured by dipping the leaf of such-and-such a plant in calva and placing it on the affected part. An old countryman even told me that when taken with a fever as a child, he was ordered by his doctor (not Doctor Marais) to go to bed, drink calvados and watch his bedpost. When he could see two of them he would have had enough 'medicine' and would be well in the morning.

Certainly, that morning in René's orchard, I could sense something magical in the air. Maybe it was the calva fumes, possibly it was the magic of Normandy itself. Does it, perhaps, lie under Merlin's enchantment? Could this misty land of apples and antique customs be Avalon? That is certainly Doctor Marais' belief. Maybe it's not such a far-fetched idea as all that. It all goes back to the Celts...

"The Celts gave the tribes across the Rhine the name 'Germans'" the doctor told me, as we walked his garden one day. "Meaning close relations. Sadly for the Celts, those relations had a habit of getting rather too close."

The first major attack on Gaul had a very definite date: the last day of the year 406. In a massive assault, the Francs, Lombards, Burgundians and Goths crossed the frozen Rhine. Meanwhile, the Angles and Saxons were attacking Britain.

Roman rule had already cracked once in Britain. Legions had been removed from the island forty year earlier to take part in one of Rome's many civil wars, allowing the Picts to cross Hadrian's Wall and burn York. Britain had been saved at that time by reinforcements from the continent. This time the attacks from the sea were widespread and co-ordinated.

"The barbarians drive us to the sea and the sea drives us back to the barbarians" cried the Britons to Rome. There was to be no relief. It was the end. Four years later Rome herself fell to the Goths.

The Celts faced an enemy with whom co-existence was not possible: flight or slavery were the only alternatives. Attacked by the Anglo-Saxons, the Britons fled west, north and south, into Somerset, Wales and Northumbria, and in huge numbers to the semi-island of the Cherbourg Peninsula, where their ancestors had defied the Romans.

It was an exodus. Geoffrey of Monmouth (who is admittedly not the most reliable of sources) says that half the Britons fled across the sea. From there they moved south and west. There were so many of them that they called their new land Little Britain (now Brittany).

Although the two Celtic groups have been separated for a thousand years, the links remain. Milizac, Sizun, Penarros, Kervezec, Carnac and St Maude are in Brittany, not Cornwall (the Breton and Cornish landscapes are remarkably similar). The Bretons of Petite Bretagne can still converse with their Celtic cousins in Grande Bretagne. They share the same customs and folklore, especially the Arthurian tales.

Arthur was a king of the Britons, and his kingdom spanned the Channel. Stories of the good king, Guinevere, Merlin and the court are common in Brittany. Certain woods and castles are named as those where their deeds took place. Was Arthur, as has been suggested, the king who saved the Britons from extinction by the Anglo-Saxons? Did he do the same for the Bretons against the Franks?

Doctor Marais is sure that Arthur is part of our common culture. "Your tales tell of a British king who was finally borne from a Somerset battlefield, wounded but alive, to the safety of an island across the water. Could not Avalon, the island of mists, marshes, mistletoe and apples, have been the Cherbourg Peninsula? Perhaps from here the Once and Future King was carried at last deeper into British lands. To Brittany. To sleep there with his court in Arthur's Cave in Arthur's Camp, between the Pool of the Boars and the Trembling Rock."

If so, his sleep must have been sorely troubled by the Franks, and in particular by Charlemagne, who, in the year 799, subdued even Brittany.

"Under Charlemagne" the doctor explained, "the Franks pushed out in all directions. To the south they took much of Italy, to the north the lands of many German tribes. These tribes he converted to Christianity, but not a brand that the modern day church would endorse. Charlemagne's was an Old Testament Christianity. Those who would not submit to it were slaughtered, their lands confiscated, their families sold into slavery and their homes put to the torch.

The refugees from The Religion of Love fled into Denmark, Norway and Sweden. Then they took to the sea to find new homes and revenge themselves on the Christians. Charlemagne achieved his ambition to be Emperor of Rome but at a terrible price for the Celts - amongst others. He unleashed the Vikings."

Calvados usually had a part in Norman tales. Perhaps it has a part in this one too. Calvados, like whisky, means 'water of life'. Is it a Celtic survival? Those red-headed individualists with their poetry, art, and wild temper were as fond of a tipple as their descendants are today.

Not all spirits are liquid. When I was stationed at RAF Conningsby in Lincolnshire, the ghosts who were supposed to haunt a hangar on the airfield were a frequent topic of discussion in the airmen's mess. I think they were the crew of a target-marking aircraft which crashed while taking off for a raid on Germany. None of we airmen were the least afraid of ghosts ...until the time came to do guard duty at night.

Can such things be? The only time I heard tell of a ghost in France, it was an English one. Its haunt was a big, old, rambling hotel, an ancient coaching house which had gradually annexed half a street.

Additions and alterations had made it into a fascinating labyrinth; a warren of staircases, corridors and rooms which wandered over arches and courtyards and threw out wings at right-angles into the gardens behind. The gardens, with their ancient greenhouses, old stables and clumps of overgrown laurels, held their own fascination.

I 'took on' the place one sunny day in late autumn. After the viewing I sat in the breakfast room with the owners, who were on the point of retiring. I was served tea. This time, for a mercy, it was not some horrid 'tisane' of cherry or raspberry leaves, but honest-to-goodness tea with proper milk (not UHT), a unique occurence in France. The breakfast room had an English feel to it. The plates around the walls were of willow-pattern and crazed with age. Madame saw me looking at them and smiled.

"They were the Milord's plates."

I settled comfortably back in my chair for a story. And I got it.

"They say," began Madame, "that during the last century an Englishman, a rich one, had the wing that runs into the rose garden. He is supposed to have lived there for years with his own cook and servant. His hobby was photography and he used to develop his photographs up in the attics above that part of the house. One day he was found hanging up there. Yes, Monsieur, he finished himself off! The attic has the reputation of being haunted."

"Have you seen the ghost?" I asked.

"Oh no, Monsieur" she said hastily. "I do not believe in such nonsense!"

"And the plates?"

She frowned. "That's the funny thing, Monsieur. We thought it was just a story, you know, until a few years back the roof started to leak. We got a man in to look at it and it needed quite a bit of work. When finally it was done, my husband went up to check the job."

Her husband nodded.

Madame continued: "He found several crates up there and, as he has a bad back, Pierre asked the workman to bring them down for him. The roofer was in a bit of a hurry that evening and the cases were awkward, so he only managed two of them. He was to carry down the others when he came back to present his bill. Well, he never did come back, because about a week later he fell from a roof, and the poor man was killed." She paused for my reaction.

"And the boxes?"

"Well, Monsieur, we opened them up. One was full of plates: those you see on the walls here. Our visitors always admire them. Once we had an English guest who told us they were valuable."

The hotel cat rubbed against my leg. I bent to stroke her. "And the other box?"

"That was full of square glass plates. Dark they were, smoked I suppose. He must have used them for his photography."

"What happened to them?"

Madame turned to her husband, who took up the story: "I used them in the greenhouses. Some of them are still there."

I took a drink of tea and questioned Madame further: "And the rest of the crates in the attic, did you have them brought down too?"

"Well no, Monsieur..." She looked slightly abashed. "We've never been up there since. It's all nonsense, of course, but you know..."

I did know.

A few weeks later I had the chance to show the place off to a couple who were looking to buy a house. The couple, whom I will call Mr and Mrs Lucas, were very well dressed, drove a very expensive car and had a very odd brief. They wanted to "spend some money fast." A lot of money. They were looking to buy a 'character' place. I showed them several expensive houses over a period of two days but nothing seemed to suit them.

I formed the impression during that couple of days that there was something false about Mr and Mrs Lucas. Maybe my misgivings were simply due to the incident at lunch on the first day...

We had agreed that we would all have the same meal and split the bill. As usual in France, the meat came on the plates and the vegetables separately. There were twelve potatoes. Mrs Lucas politely took three and handed the dish to me. I took a further three and passed the dish to Mr Lucas. With a convulsive jerk of his fork, he scooped the remaining six potatoes onto his plate. Mr Lucas was the Six Potato Man.

One of the few things that the agency had thought it necessary to teach me was how to hold on to customers: "If you're showing them property they can't go and see other agents". There are limits, however, to this approach. The old hotel was my last throw. The owners had fled south for the winter and the hotel was shuttered up when we visited it. I went from room to room and wing to wing throwing open the shutters.

Mr and Mrs Lucas seemed particularly interested in the china in the breakfast room, so I told them about the Milord. Afterwards they asked me to identify the Rose Garden Wing and the entrance to the attic. I did so. In the same corridor was a lumber room in which a ladder was stored, doubtless the same one that had been used by the unfortunate roofer.

Finally it was time to shut up and leave. I was uncertain what the Lucas's were about, but it didn't seem to be buying property, so I was very surprised when they expressed an interest in having a second look at the hotel on the following day. They insisted, however, on bringing their own car and meeting me there. That was fine by me; they could pay for their own petrol for a change.

When I arrived at the hotel the next day, the Lucas's were waiting for me. We began the long trek from wing to wing and corridor to corridor. Perhaps I had misjudged my customers, for they seemed remarkably interested in the place. After a few minutes Mr Lucas excused himself to visit the toilet. While he was away his wife submitted me to a barrage of questions on hotel management which I was singularly unqualified to answer.

As time dragged by and Mr Lucas had not reappeared, I began to express uneasiness. Mrs Lucas, however, did not seem at all worried. Perhaps he had got lost in the rambling place, maybe he was looking at other rooms; I was not to worry about him. She continued to ply me with questions.

After an hour she finally agreed that her husband's extended absence did seem a trifle odd, and that perhaps we should look for him. It would be better, she suggested, were we to separate. Casually, she indicated her preferred route. Perhaps I would be so good as to try the opposite direction? By this time I had my suspicions that Mrs Lucas knew precisely where to find the Six Potato Man.

I knew the hotel better than she and by taking a different route to the Rose Garden Wing, reached the attic corridor only marginally behind her. As I had suspected, the lumber room ladder had been placed to give access to the attic. At that moment, the trapdoor of the attic rose by a couple of inches, hesitated a second, then dropped. I coughed. Mrs Lucas turned, the blood draining from her cheeks. She staggered out of the way.

I climbed the ladder and pushed up the trapdoor. An extraordinary sight met my eyes. Mr Lucas was in shirtsleeves, absolutely filthy and obviously exhausted. His face was pale and streaked by rivulets of sweat. His trousers were ripped. But it was his hands that shocked me. The fingers were a bloody mess.

"Christ!" he said weakly.

Mr Lucas had, he told me, decided to look in the attic to see if there was any truth in the old story. He had climbed in and the trapdoor had fallen shut behind him; how, he could not imagine. Since then he had been trying to prise it up again but it was too heavy. Each time it had risen a little way and then fallen back. He was utterly spent.

Had the ghost dropped the trap? Spirits are not usually credited with performing physical feats but this one seemed to be exceptional. Who else could have stacked the pile of willow-pattern plates at the foot of the ladder leading up to the attic?

"All reason is against it, and all belief for it" commented Doctor Johnson, on belief in the supernatural. There can be few better times to touch on the ultimate mystery than when sharing a bottle of calvados in front of a log fire in Normandy.

CHATEAU DE PIROU

The Viking storm.
From Duke Rollo to Hugh the Bull Slayer.
A house by the sea. The coefficient.
Shellfish, shrimps and soda-pop.

The Normans are, just as the English, a people of the sea. Of course, we share more or less the same hotch-potch ancestry. We owe our common love of the sea to the Vikings. Those Sea Wolves from Denmark and Norway spread terror along both sides of the Channel. In France and in Britain the identical prayer was offered up by the Christians: "From the fury of the Northmen, good Lord deliver us."

To English, French and Celt, the Lord turned a deaf ear. In one of the most chilling passages in literature, an Irish priest recorded:

"Although there were an hundred hard-steeled iron heads on one neck, and an hundred sharp, never-rusting brazen tongues in every head, and an hundred garrulous, loud, unceasing voices from every tongue, they could not recount what the people of Ireland, young and old, men and women, suffered from these ruthless, wrathful, foreign, purely pagan people."

Ireland was not alone in her woe. In the year 851, the Northmen burned both London and Paris.

The Vikings were hard. They believed that man could rely on no-one but himself and scorned pity. It would have been a weakness in their harsh world where only the strongest could survive. Only the strength which Thor had given them could be trusted.

Their religion taught them that the maidens of Valhalla awaited those who fell in battle. They grimly boasted that wherever they went the raven followed. They fought, according to those they assaulted, recklessly, madly, intoxicated by pure blood-lust, laughing at hurts taken and hewing down all those who opposed them.

Such men were not easy to stand against and they had the benefit of mobility. If their attack failed, they formed a shield-ring of axes and hacked their way back to their boats, only to land somewhere else along the coast. Alcuin of York, adviser to Charlemagne, wrote: "Never before has such terror appeared in Britain as we have suffered from a pagan race, nor was it thought that such an inroad from the sea could be made."

Above all, the Vikings hated Christianity. At Peterborough, a single Viking is said to have killed eighty-four monks with his own hand. They struck Northern England in massive force, the great library of York blazing to their torches.

Where first they plundered they later settled. The Anglo-Saxons tried to buy them off with gold - Danegeld - but the Norse and Danish wolves not only bit the hands that fed them, they went for the throat. They meant to have England.

Army after Viking army was thrown against Alfred's Wessex, the last English kingdom to hold out against them. They failed. But they had already gained much. In 878 the northern half of England became the Norse kingdom of Northumbria, while the East Midlands became The Danelaw.

Across the Channel the Britons (I will call them Bretons from now on) had regained independence and much of their land from the Franks. Now they were attacked from the sea and through the confused channels of the Carentan Marshes. To the Vikings, the marshes formed both a roadway and a barrier against attack from the south.

At first they built themselves fortified towers next to the sea, such as the magical castle of Pirou, north of Coutances. In towers such as this they stashed their loot from their raids on Britain and France. Then they began to move into and settle lands further from the coast. The Celtic life-line between Little Britain and Great Britain was cut.

"We tried to stop them" said Doctor Marais in his study.

The doctor had a way of speaking that always made me think that he had been present at whatever event he was describing. He could conjure up Roman generals and Viking longboats as readily as a magician can produce doves.

"There were look-out towers over the marshes. But the ships had too shallow a draught, and the guards couldn't be everywhere. The berserkers got through at a hundred points." He stopped to reflect for a moment, then corrected himself: "But of course 'we' did not try to stop them. Rather my Gaulish and Frankish ancestors tried to fight off my Danish, Norse, Angle and Saxon ancestors - oh yes, they were here too."

The closely related invaders called themselves the Northmen. The Francs, like their descendants the French, found it hard to get their tongues around the 'th' sound, so they called the invaders Normans.

In the year 911, the Franks were forced to make the same concessions as the English had made, and gave up land to the invaders. The Danish and Norse settlements were united to form the Duchy of Normandy. It was no more than the recognition of a fait accompli. The Normans had to be accommodated.

The king of the Franks, glad to see the berserkers turn their rage in a direction other than his own, also accorded the Normans the 'right' to pillage Brittany. The first Norman Duke was Rollo the Raider. The closing event of his investiture as Duke shows the true nature of the relationship:

"There remained one act. The homage. It was necessary for the Northman to kneel, place his hands in the king's and bend and kiss the sovereign's foot. This Rollo refused to do. He signalled one of his men to take his place for the formal ritual. The man took hold of the royal ankle right enough but instead of bending to it, lifted it to his lips, tipping the king and his throne backwards. The whole of Saint-Clair-sur-Epte echoed to the howl of Viking laughter at the spectacle of the Frankish king with his trotters in the air."

The Northmen adopted the language and religion of France, although they gave many of their own harsh words to the language - especially maritime ones such as 'houle' for a sea swell, 'varech' (wrack) for seaweed, the names of the points of the compass and many shipping terms.

Duke Rollo was a pagan converted to Christianity. But he was also a man who knew how to hedge his bets. On his deathbed, it is said, he ordered a hundred pounds of gold to be spent on masses in the Christian churches. He also ordered that a hundred Christian prisoners be beheaded as a sacrifice to Thor...

The Franks did not take the foundation of Normandy lightly. They launched attack after attack against the invaders, as did all the peoples from whom the Vikings had stolen land; the Flambards, the Burgundians and the Bretons. But in vain. The Normans were not to be removed from their conquests ...but the attacks did give them pause for thought.

Hemmed in as were the Normans by enemies, they sought a safer and more easily protected retreat. In the year 1031, Duke Robert, William the Conqueror's father, launched an invasion fleet against England. The wind was against the Normans and took them instead to Jersey. Nothing daunted, they sailed on to pillage Brittany.

As well as guarding and extending their borders, the Normans had enemies to deal with at home. The Norsemen of the Cherbourg Peninsula did not bow easily to the ever more restrictive powers of the Duke. Nor did they welcome

Christianity. They launched an army against the Duke. They were heavily defeated.

Many of the survivors took ship and sailed south to serve as mercenaries in Italy. First they went in dribs and drabs but soon they were flocking south in their thousands. They joined the Greek army attacking the Moslems in Sicily. Among that multi-national force the Normans found fellow Vikings, the Varengians, who had sailed from the Baltic.

The Norsemen showed all the qualities of their ancestors, fighting like devils and showing little respect for their paymasters. The Greeks feared them greatly and decided to teach them a lesson, once and for all. To this end they made an example of a Norman troublemaker and publicly whipped him. The Normans promptly revolted and joined with the Varengians to fight on their own account, depriving the Greek army of its shock troops.

"At the head of this Norse contingent was William Iron Arm, oldest of the dozen sons of Tancred of Hauteville - near Coutances," explained the doctor. "The Greeks sent emissaries to parley with the rebels. The Northmen thought it high time the Greeks learned respect, so Hugh the Bull Slayer, a giant even among the Vikings, played his party piece. He seized the bridle of the messenger's horse and, with a single blow between the eyes, dropped the beast stone dead."

The Normans rapidly took the heel of Italy, with more of Tancred's sons setting up as princes.

The doctor poked the fire and added a log. Night had fallen. It was cold. Bitterly cold. He stared pensively into the flames.

"The Pope didn't think much of those birds of prey who carved out huge slices of Italy for themselves as if by divine right. He took to the field against them at the head of an army. The army was defeated and the Pope captured. The pontiff made the best of a bad job, as had every other ruler who had been faced with these sea people who were spreading along the coasts of Europe like a canker. Their very names, William Iron Arm, Hugh the Bull Slayer, Sweyn Bluebeard, Eric

Bloodaxe, brought fear. His Holiness blessed the new Norman state to his south and made its king a Defender of the Faith and an ally. He badly needed allies. There were three different claimants to his throne."

Norman fortunes were on the up and up. They had married into the royal household of England and under William Normandy became the best administered state in Western Europe.

"How much of one's later life can be ascribed to the events of childhood?" mused the doctor. "William, who was only seven when his father died, had a turbulent upbringing. Many attempts were made to get rid of him and his closest advisers were murdered, one of them in William's own bedchamber. He quickly learnt to trust no-one but himself."

The doctor moved his chair yet closer to the fire. "William grew to be a ruthless man, a politician of genius and a great military leader. He needed to be all those things, for the Franks had not forgotten him. In the ten years before the Conquest they twice sent armies to crush the upstarts. In vain. We waited until the invaders passed by, then sallied forth and cut them to pieces. The marshes, the mists and the bocage were our allies. This secret land with its tortured lanes, its hidden valleys, its woods and fogs, has always been ideal guerilla country. Even so, we had many enemies and few friends. To grow we needed a secure base. England."

I had the strange feeling that were I to venture out into the iron-hard night, beneath the silent majesty of the winter stars, I might well come across a dishevelled party of Vikings, huddled around a campfire in Madame Marais' immaculate herbaceous borders.

England had been fought over by Norse, Danes and English. Finally (and by general consent) Canute, a Dane, was crowned. Thus was the land united. The crown remained Danish until Canute's last son died "as he stood at his drink at Lambeth". Although the Danes felt the crown should have remained theirs, it passed back to the English: to King Edward, a gentle but ineffectual man whose mother had been

Norman.

England was a rich prize. The Danes meant to have the crown back. William's father had already tried to invade her; his son intended to do the job properly. After Edward's death the highest civilisation in Europe was to feel again the Viking double-edged axe.

From Wareham to Warsaw, the Viking story has sent echoes across the centuries. When I was a boy in York I would press my face against the shop window of Cravens' chocolate factory and look longingly at the sweets. Cravens was built on a marshy bit of land hard by the river Foss. Now the factory has been ripped down and the site excavated. The archaeologists unearthed a Viking settlement, much of it wonderfully preserved.

The site has been opened as 'The World of the Vikings' and is now one of York's many tourist attractions. Such mounds of oyster-shells were found there as to be an embarrassment. They were sold off at ten pence a time. It would have amazed the Vikings (and the Normans) but I reckon they were good value at that. Oyster-shells are immensely satisfying to handle. Forget the clicking and clacking of worry beads - try an oyster-shell instead.

It is doubtful whether the Vikings ever used oyster-shells (or anything else) to lower their blood pressure. They were far more
interested in raising it.

Beside being warlike, the Vikings had other distinguishing features. As the 'Histoire de la Normandie' has it:

> "They had all the qualities - and all the faults - that can be found today in the markets and fairs of Normandy. They were intelligent, stubborn and drove a hard bargain. Sometimes they were crafty."

These legacies are obvious not only in Normandy, but on the eastern seaboard of England too. I'm not sure how the East Anglians sum up this mixed blessing, but in Yorkshire we say:

> "Hear all, see all, say nowt,
> Drink all, eat all, pay nowt,
> And if tha does owt for nowt,
> Do it for thissen."

These days the strength of the gale that blows through the Channel is not measured by a piece of knotted rope flung from the stern of a longship, but by the Beaufort Scale. If a similar scale existed for the bravery required to eat shellfish, an oyster, which one has merely to open, disengage from the shell and swallow alive, would score five. Whelks would score eight.

This momentous realisation came to me in a garage-cum-workshop where two girls were busily washing oysters. A notice behind them proclaimed that you didn't have to be mad to work there, but it helped. An adjoining room was full of buckets and baskets of mussels, whelks, lobsters, winkles, crabs and spider crabs.

René and Therese had invited us to their seaside house to celebrate Bastille Day, and René had taken us to buy some shellfish. He tried without success to interest us in the whelks - a kind of sea snail, a mound of which were wriggling their rubbery yellow feet in the air. He bought some oysters and mussels and we left.

René and Therese's seaside place was a ruin when they bought it. They have lovingly rebuilt it, inch by inch, including that most powerful symbol of French life, the hearth. It is a typical Norman granite fireplace with a griddle, iron fireback and cremaillere. After they had rehung the cremaillere - the ratchet toothed bar from which the cauldron hangs over the fire - they had the place blessed by the priest: a true house-warming party.

We watched the Bastille Day celebrations on television. Tanks, guns, trucks and soldiers paraded past the top brass; even (Ann swears) a rubber-suited frogman sitting to attention in a dinghy. The President, whom we might call a 'big cheese', is a 'big vegetable' to his own people. Then we ate.

The meal started with the oysters. You need an oyster knife to open an oyster. It must be inserted into the hinge at a steep angle and worked round the shell. Then, if you are brave, you will disengage the creature from its shell and swallow it raw.

Otherwise it can be drained, the shell packed with butter, parsley and chopped garlic, topped off with breadcrumbs and grilled for ten minutes. Delicious. We ate them raw, with a dressing of vinegar, chopped onion and garlic. Next came mussels. Then we had sausages, followed by chops, the last two courses grilled over the open fire.

As ever in Normandy, our meal was punctuated by cider and wine. How the French manage to match their booze to their food so expertly I don't know. But then I am a mere Horsain (foreigner). The meal was finished off with a drop of calvados. The Normans call this tot 'Le Trou Normand' (The Norman hole) when it is drunk between courses.

After we had eaten I told the tale of the spider crab which I bought in the market. Ever eager to try something new, I questioned the stall-holder closely about the edible parts and the correct way to prepare the beast. Ann boiled it and opened it up.

The inside of a spider crab is not pretty. I will not describe it in detail. Suffice it to say that if a whelk rates eight on the scale of unapproachability, the spider crab rates at least ten. We ended up by throwing it in the orchard uneaten, contenting ourselves with the claw meat. As the name 'spider crab' suggests, there is not much of that.

The French family heard out my tale in silent horror: throwing away a spider crab! It was true, then, that the English are mad! It does no harm to reinforce people's prejudices occasionally.

Then we went for a walk on the beach.

As the British have found out time and again, being first is not always to be recommended. Innovators run into all the problems. When the Victorian engineers installed the first sewage systems since the Romans, they pumped the effluent out to sea wherever possible. Many of these outfalls remain to this day (the cost of replacing them would be astronomical) and the malady lingers on...

Swimming off a Suffolk resort, I have learnt at first hand about sewage outfalls. The experience cost me a week in bed, and a sore throat for a month. A friend who lives in a remote Yorkshire seaside village has told me that the mussels there are all becoming male because of mercury pollution.

By contrast, the waters off Normandy are clean. They are shallow too, for the beaches slope very gently into the sea and there is no Continental Shelf. The sea is warm and, on the western side of the Cherbourg Peninsula, warmed further by the Gulf Stream.

These clean, warm, shallow seas are perfect for swimming and for marine life too. But, as Normandy has the highest tides in Europe, it can be a very long walk to the water's edge. Usually it is a mile between high and low water. At Gouville, the Senequet lighthouse is over two miles offshore at high tide but high and dry at the lowest tide.

The huge, rich, foreshore is littered with shells and its potential has not been missed by the French. It is heavily farmed. On the beaches, board-walks are suspended between lines of stakes. There are literally thousands of these trestles along the coast. They are oyster beds. Oysters are cheap in France. They are cultured in open-mesh sacks which are tied to the trestles. As the tide goes out, row upon row of them are revealed, often stretching a mile into the sea.

The oyster farmers take their tractors out to the beds, haul up a few sacks and go inshore. The sacks are sorted for oysters which are ready to sell (they are four or five years old before they are big enough), the empty shells discarded and the smaller ones re-sorted and replaced on the trestles.

A quarter of all the mussels and oysters eaten in France come from the Norman coast. None are ever stolen. I came near to it one day, but I had not counted with the mystical rapport between the 'ostreiculteur' and his oysters. I found a sack of oysters at Arromanches, among the wreckage of the Mulberry harbour (of which more later). The sack had obviously been washed up.

It was a January day and the beach was deserted. Our car was parked a couple of hundred yards away. I was tempted. Are not such things flotsam (or possibly jetsam); gifts from the sea and the property of whoever discovers them?

Lucifer was winning the struggle for my soul when a fast-moving speck appeared far away across the sands. Soon it became recognisable as a white van. Finally it screeched to a halt in front of us. The driver got out, chucked the sack in the back of the van and drove off without a word.

The sea never sleeps. It is, of course, the moon that keeps it on the move. The French give a measurement to this tidal range. They call it the coefficient. The nearer is the moon to the earth, the further does the sea come in and roll out: and the greater is the coefficient. The average coefficient is seventy-five (if there was no tide it would be zero). If there is a greater lunar pull, as happens at full moon and in spring and autumn, the coefficient rises.

The French watch the coefficient table (which is published in local newspapers and almanacs) like hawks. The higher the coefficient, the greater the number of rakes and buckets which are stowed into their Citroens and Renaults.

As low tide approaches, cars appear among the dunes and determined and begumbooted figures, festooned with their rakes and buckets, make their way to the water's edge. There they grat (scrape) earnestly with their rateaux (rakes) for shellfish. They are searching for anything; mussels, oysters, whelks, cockles - and the elusive Coque Bleu.

The Coque Bleu is a mollusc of near reverence in the family Biggins. It was René who let slip that the creature exists and hinted at its delights. It is reputedly the supreme catch of the lower shore but we have never succeeded in sampling it. Ann, who has a degree in zoology, is as puzzled by it as I am - for it figures in no dictionary, pictorial or otherwise. Nor have we found it in the shops.

For a while, I haunted the fish shops of Granville in search of it: "Got any Coque Bleu?" The owners would look at me in surprise. Inevitably they had none. They had had some last week; or they knew someone who might have some (but in fact didn't). I cast my net wider. The fish shop assistants of Coutances were less broadminded than their Granville cousins. They looked at me in much the same way as the girl on the counter at W.H. Smith's would were I to sidle up to her and say "Got any hard porn, luv?"

Eventually I gave up this full-frontal attack and began a sort of sporadic, guerilla action - hitting fish stalls on markets as occasion arose. Finally one of them - possibly alerted by the Guild of French Shellfish Sellers (Manche chapter) about my activities - put me out of my misery. The Coque Bleu can not be sold by fishmongers, for they are not caught commercially and the fishmonger's licence does not cover the sale of non-commercially caught fish. It seems that I will never make the acquaintanceship of this reputedly delightful creature.

The Biggins family are people of the sea; both through ancestry and inclination. After a day at the seaside comes a soak. By eight 'o clock at night the bathroom is free again. The only evidence the children have left behind them is a twisting trace of sand in the bottom of the bath, a grainy floor and a 'Beano' comic on top of the toilet. Sneaking into David's room reveals a rosy-cheeked infant dead to the world with his arm around his teddy bear. He dreams, perhaps, of crabs and ice-creams, shrimps and soda-pop. Ann stretches.

The sea, the eternal sea; thou destroyer and healer. Soon, lulled by the memory of the roar and undertow of its waves, we, too, will sleep.

MONT ST MICHEL

Frontier land. The eye of the storm
The cigogne. Quicksands. Bartering a bidet.

Beyond the river Couesnon lies the land of bagpipes and cabers, mists and moorland, castles and Celts. Brittany.

The Couesnon runs into the Bay of Mont St Michel, a strange land won from the sea, where ancient villages twist their way to (artificial?) church-topped mounds.

William passed this way regularly. He is said to have feared the bay far more than he did the Bretons. What are now poplar-bordered fields were in his day tidal swampland with slicks of evil grey mud that swallowed men and beasts. The Bayeux Tapestry shows the Duke crossing the bay with Harold, the man who he was later to kill for his crown. They were heading westward to fight at the Breton fortresses of Dol de Bretagne and Dinan. The crossing was tricky. The tapestry shows Harold dragging his men out of the quaking filth.

William was no more loved beyond the Couesnon than he was to be in England. On one of his campaigns the defenders of a besieged town poked fun at the trade of his grandfather, a leather maker. They hung cow skins from the walls and jeered at the attacker, "Hides for the tanner!" William didn't see the joke. When the town fell, he flayed some defenders alive and cut off the hands and feet of others.

The Bay is used to the passing of armies. At least one of them will stay there forever - in the German ossuary at Huisnes sur Mer, where are twelve thousand German soldiers. Here lies a private, born on the 13th of August 1924, died on the 8th of August 1944. Dead before his twentieth birthday. Cannon fodder. "Wasted" as the Americans termed similar soldiers in Vietnam.

How did he die? In some fighter-bomber attack on the beaches? Or perhaps he was one of the lads buried by the owner of one of 'my' houses. That old chap told me that the Americans had taken eleven days to advance from the next village, three miles away. His father's fields had been littered with German dead after the fierce fighting. The owner had been a boy then, and the Americans had ordered him to bury the dead. He pointed out the places where he had scooped out the graves: "There, and there, and there."

The floor of his house seemed in unusually good condition. It had been laid in 1945. A German shell from an anti-tank gun on the ridge in front had come through the front door and blown the heart out of the house. The whole of the refugee family who had been sheltering there at the time had been killed. The old countryman swallowed. Even after fifty years the memory came near to making him cry.

"It was terrible. Parents, children. Dead. Then there were the Germans I had to bury. I thought they were big men then, for I was sixteen and already thought myself a man. Now that I have children and grandchildren of my own, it seems to me that the soldiers were little more than kids themselves. Children with guns, and heads stuffed full of nonsense."

The Germans that he buried were dug up again and moved to the cemetery at Huisnes. There they lie in peace with their comrades, as so many warriors lie in Normandy. From the cemetery one can see Mont St Michel, rising in incomparable beauty through the morning mists.

When the Bretons are being polite (relationships between Breton and Norman have not always been of the best), they say that Mont St Michel is only Norman because of the way the Couesnon happened to be flowing on the day the boundary was drawn. Looking at the river today it's difficult to see what they mean.

But the Bay wasn't always the way it is now. Until a century ago the Couesnon was constantly changing its course. Its channel and quicksand banks snaked across country and sometimes drowned whole villages (it took Dutch engineers to tame it, which is why, no doubt, the reclaimed lands are called 'polders').

The Mount itself stands at the end of a ribbon-causeway and hangs between the blue immensities of sea and sky. It was built upon because Anselm, bishop of Avranches (which overlooks the Bay) was visited in his sleep by St Michael, who ordered the Bishop to construct a church on the granite island. The Bishop took no heed. The Saint visited him a second time. The Bishop again ignored him (his claim not to believe in divine visitation must surely be unique in a clergyman of his era).

After the Saint's third visit, when he struck the dim prelate on the head to drive home his point, Anselm finally got the message and began to build. The Bishop's dented skull is still to be seen in the cathedral at Avranches.

Mont St Michel was not only a temple of the spirit but a military fortress too; an impregnable storehouse of men and arms, ready to be catapulted against the enemy, whether he be Breton, French, Burgundian or English. Great walls rise sheer from the mud and the sea itself was its moat, for it could only be approached at low tide over twisting and changing paths through the marshes and quicksands.

The first church was built on the summit. It was over-built and lay hidden for a thousand years as cyclopean walls were thrown up to construct an infinitely complex and interleaved edifice. 'The Marvel', a palace of corridors, pillars, staircases, chapels and guesthouses took over the upper part of the Mount. Its breath-taking culmination is the Abbey at the summit, topped by the gilded statue of St Michel standing sentinel above his bay.

Just inside the first gateway stand two cannons, with barrels large enough to take my son David (to his delight). These are guns abandoned in the marshes by the English in 1434 when their siege of the Mount failed - as it always failed, for this was the one spot in Normandy that we never took. The eye of the storm.

After passing through two more gateways, the narrow and twisting street climbs to the Abbey. Up and up. The ancient gabled houses lean towards each other in the companionship of half a millennium.

David loves Mont St Michel for what the shops sell: "Choc bars, plunger sucker guns, handcluffs (he means handcuffs), truncheons, cosmic monsters, robots, models of Mont St Michel, picture frames, snowstorms, toy swords and helmets, cameras that squirt water, other cameras that when you click them you see a photo of Mont St Michel, trumpets with a bit of string on them." He also loves the reproduction armour and maces and crossbows and swords which the shops sell.

Ann loves Mont St Michel for the narrow little alleyways, the roofs with their wooden tiles, the cloister in the Abbey which looks out over the sea, and the seafood. A few years ago she made the mistake of ordering fruit de mer at a restaurant there. The plate was covered five deep in shellfish. The dastardly waiter had maliciously omitted to supply a winkle-picker.

For a student of humanity of a sadistic bent, the incident doubtless offered interesting possibilities. Would the English realise that anything was missing? Even if they did, would a member of that self-effacing race have the temerity to ask for a replacement? How would they phrase their request?

The proceedings were watched with interest and malevolence by a very fat and very blonde family of unknown nationality. I took some delight, when asked by Ann for help, to crack the crab in their direction.

Alice likes the walk along the ramparts with its stairs and ancient towers.

I love all those things, as well as the plaster gargoyles that you can buy and the barkers who try to persuade you to go and see prison cells and 'dioramas' of the bay (whatever they might be). I love looking up at 'Le Merveil' and speculating what it would be like to have free run of the place.

I like to sit on the wall in the Abbey Garden and pore over 'We built Mont St Michel', a masterpiece of a guide book which gives an insight into the problems of the medieval engineers and architects. I lose myself in its beautiful drawings and understand (for a brief moment) the complex world of stone; its stresses, opposing forces and lateral and vertical pressures.

Gradually the story of the abbey above the sea unfolds: the triumphs and disasters of a thousand years (various bits of the Marvel have fallen off from time to time). The book gives me a double dose of pleasure. It is high art explaining high art.

I believe that there are people who are quite unmoved by Mont St Michel. It takes all sorts. To me the place is an irresistible mixture of the eternal and the transitory. What is not so wonderful about the Mount is its popularity. You stand a fair chance of being turned back in summer if you arrive too late; and even if you aren't, you may spend an hour in a traffic jam.

The jam continues inside. The single street is a nightmarish mass of bodies. If you are canny you either get there before eleven or take one of the narrow stairs onto the ramparts and climb the hill that way, deprived of the joys of tat but with sublime views of the Bay.

Mont St Michel is much less of an island than it once was. Breakwaters and land reclamation have advanced the shore two or three miles towards it. It is connected to the mainland by a causeway which is never covered by the sea. That causeway has stopped the flow of water around the island. The bay is silting up.

That silt almost caused my downfall. One Wednesday I took Alice with me to 'take on' a property in the Bay. It was a smallholding of thirty acres - the farmhouse itself being a fine, solid building of Norman granite. While Alice stayed with Madame and played with a white kitten, the farmer, a very affable man, showed me over his land, which was in two parcels.

He asked me for a valuation. I hummed and hawed. I had no idea. However, I remembered reading an article in the barber's which said that the price of agricultural land had slipped again - for the fourteenth successive year - and now stood at 20,000 to 30,000 francs a hectare. I gave the farmer a valuation based on the lower figure. He seemed surprised.

"But, monsieur, this is silt - the finest land in the world for carrots and potatoes, and that is how my notaire has valued it."

I hastily revised my opinion.

The farmer could justly have accused me of incompetence but he forgave me. We went back to his house for a calvados. Had I heard about the cigogne which was nesting just down the road? The bird was normally unknown hereabouts - did we have them in England? Cigogne? I supposed him to mean 'cygne' - swan. Yes, of course we did, they were common in my country. The farmer nodded. It was a huge nest, ornithologists had come from all over France to see it.

I began to wonder. Do swans have nests? I had never seen one. Noting my baffled look, the farmer gave me directions to the nesting site, and Alice and I set off. We got lost. The farmer must have anticipated that we would, for he arrived on his tractor and 'guided us in'. Down the road, in the crown of a pollarded willow, was a great nest of stick and straw - and on the nest was an enormous bird - a stork.

The family Biggins visited the Mount on the day of the highest tide of the century (coefficient 119). The four of us stood with hundreds of others on the causeway and watched as the sea pushed its outriders and jellyfish up the river Couesnon; watched as the Couesnon disappeared under the waves.

Soon the water covered the footbridge which leads to the gateway onto the Mount. A small door was opened at the base of one of the flanking towers, large enough to take just two at a time. The crowd fluxed about it as darkness fell, those on the walls above bantering good naturedly with those that waited to go in. Behind the Mount's great protecting wall the lights of the shops shone warmly on the steep and winding street to the Abbey, as they have for centuries.

As we walked back up the curving causeway we turned to see the Mount reflected from walls to summit in the calm water; the perfect jigsaw puzzle. If this poem to the Almighty can move today's car-bound visitor as it does, how must it have affected the pilgrim who journeyed on foot for weeks and months to see it?

We have left a little of ourselves in the Bay of Mont St Michel. Our bidet to be exact.

It all began when I went to 'take on' a house in those polders won back from the sea. Set back from a minor road and quite alone, it was a small place, consisting of a bedroom, a kitchen/living room and a lumber room. The furniture was immaculate, and typically Norman; a beautiful and highly polished antique oak cupboard with inset brass, a Norman grandfather clock, a massive oak table, and the most solid wooden bed I have ever seen. The furnishings were probably worth more than the house.

On the mantlepiece were faded photographs of a man in First World War uniform, a lady in Edwardian clothes and a wedding group dated nineteen thirty-nine. Brass shell-cases reflected the firelight, giving the room a homely atmosphere.

There was a slight untidiness about the house, as if it missed a woman's touch. A 'pain de campagne' - a heavy, stodgy loaf, lay partly cut on the table. The kitten had deposited a dead vole on the hearth. Monsieur explained that his wife had passed away the year before and that he was now selling-up to move in with his daughter.

The ritual was the same as ever; the strong black coffee with a tot of calvados, the box of sugar lumps, the little biscuits with serrated edges. Monsieur was voluble and I sensed that he probably didn't have many people to talk to, so I lingered longer than usual over the calvados and coffee.

The old fellow had seen many changes in the Bay. When he was a boy there had been a railway to Mont St Michel, and many people had arrived on horseback and on foot. Now it was all cars and coaches.

There had been more people in the commune in those days. Why, his mother had brought up four children in this one bedroom cottage! Could Monsieur believe it? Monsieur shook his head. Did Monsieur know about the tides in the bay? Monsieur did not.

The old man smiled in satisfaction and refilled my coffee cup. His hand was shaky. The highest tides in Europe they were: fifteen kilometres between the highest and the lowest. Fifteen kilometres! Could Monsieur understand that? And the sands that stretch for ever. He looked into the fire.

"The tides, Monsieur, are fast. There have been many tragedies because of them. Many tragedies."

Would a man have trouble outrunning the rising tide? His face lit up.

"Bien sur, Monsieur. It would be totally impossible. Progress is always slow, for the sands are never firm; and then there are the quicksands. If they do not swallow you completely, they will hold you back so that you cannot escape the tide. Besides, the sands are not perfectly flat. The sea can outflank a man before he knows it and he is left on a sandbar waiting for the end. It has happened many times."

I asked him about the quicksands.

"They are foul, Monsieur, and very dangerous. They are neither sea nor land but they have currents, slow currents, that move constantly. Only those who watch it and know its ways can safely cross the bay."

Before the causeway was built, the pilgrims, he told me, always had guides. Nor must I think it safer today. Had I not heard of the man who only last year had tried to drive around the base of the Mount in his new Range Rover? The car sank without trace.

"Parisian I expect" the old fellow chuckled gleefully.

I don't know how we got on to the subject of the bidet that Ann wanted to replace with a toilet; but he was very interested. Was the bidet in good condition? Did I want to sell it? The answer to both questions was yes, although I could not see what he could possibly want with a bidet, having survived for probably eighty years without even a toilet. He didn't want it for himself, he explained; his daughter had always expressed an interest in owning such a thing. If I bought a customer to see the house, why not bring the bidet at the same time? I agreed.

He was a fascinating old boy and a real raconteur. I listened to him for two hours as he told me stories about the bay; about the fogs, about the Silent Man, about the tragedies. By the time I left I was enveloped in a calvados glow and inclined to look over my shoulder.

Some weeks later I did take a customer to see the house. She was a little surprised when I stopped en-route to load the bidet in the boot, so I told her the story. While my customer took a second look around the house on her own, I showed the bidet to the owner. He was obviously impressed: how much did I want for it? I was no expert in bidet pricing: how about one hundred francs? Monsieur frowned. The price was not correct. I was a little taken aback. It had seemed reasonable enough to me.

He shook his head slowly: "The correct price, Monsieur, is two hundred francs."

An amiable sort of reverse-bargaining began. Was that not too much? No, his daughter was rich. She could afford it. Besides, it was the correct price. I didn't take much convincing. He smiled and dropped his voice confidentially.

"Perhaps, Monsieur, you would like to do the deal a little

differently?" I looked at him in silence. He pushed back his chair, stood up and moved towards the door. I followed him to an outhouse, where were several huge oak barrels and perhaps a dozen racks of bottles. Calvados. He pulled one out.

"Instead of money, perhaps a bottle of the twelve-year-old would be more to your taste?"

I had tasted his twelve-year-old - a pearl of a calvados. I nodded. He put it into my hands and turned back to his racks.

"But it is not enough. Perhaps Monsieur would like a bottle of something a little special too, a bottle of my father's?"

From the dustiest of the racks he selected a cobwebbed bottle, corked and sealed with wax.

"This calvados has a history, Monsieur. When the Americans were coming this way, the Germans told us to be ready for evacuation. My father knew what that meant. He buried all his 'calva'. The area changed hands several times. When we finally returned it proved that my father had been correct. Three thousand litres of cider had been drunk. Not a drop was left. But they had not found the calva. This is one of the last bottles. It's good stuff."

I had no doubt of it; but wouldn't he rather keep it for himself? The old man smiled a little sadly.

"I think my calva drinking days are few now, Monsieur."

Three thousand litres of cider must have made for a real running battle.

My generous friend has sold his house and is now comfortably installed with his daughter. He has taken on a new lease of life in the small town where they live and can often be seen playing bowls with his friends. He is still, to my knowledge, working his way through his calvados.

A good deal more calvados is made in Normandy than is declared to the authorities. Whether it has been distilled legally or not, the powers-that-be take a dim view of it being given away. I have been given quite a few bottles in my time, usually wrapped in a newspaper and handed over with a wink. It is a sort of unofficial currency for the payment of favours, the expression of esteem, and bartering. I'm afraid it does not last long with me. The twelve-year-old that the old man gave me is long gone. The pre-war bottle, however, is a very frustrating vintage.

Calvados, like whisky, is a drink that one should imbibe in front of a fire with a friend while contemplating the universe. This bottle I can only look at. I can not bring myself to drink it.

JEUNE ELEVE

A slow learner. Playground games. School do's.
French time. Children's education.
Merci beaucoup.

They say that the best way to learn a language is to get yourself a lover; a sort of 'Nine and a Half Weeks' approach. It's probably true but unfortunately spouses take a dim view of that sort of thing, no matter how good the cause.

Still there are other ways. The adverts scream from newspapers and magazines nearly every day:

Learning French is easy!
Money back if not satisfied!

Some of the courses take three months, some three and a half weeks. The really idle can take a pill or learn it in their sleep. It can only be a matter of time before a forty-eight hour course is available.

Learning French is easy!

So why has it taken me sixteen years?

I've spent those years atoning for the fact that I didn't bother to go to school very often after the age of fourteen. I was never going to pass the exams, so why waste hours being bored by chemistry, biology or French?

I was beset by temptations. If 'Noo York, Noo York' is 'one helluva town', what about 'old' York? It was only two miles walk away. How could classrooms compete with the railway museum, castle, city walls, rivers, swimming baths, alleys and chip shops of the great and ancient city?

I ended up with few qualifications and a stinking headmaster's report. Still, it was interesting. I was in turn a milkman and a chimney sweep's assistant before joining the Royal Air Force. Afterwards I became a computer operator. It was in the first days of computing and many a slacker escaped their just deserts by getting in on the act. However, my past caught up with me when I wanted to move jobs. I needed qualifications.

Never mind, I could quickly pick up a foreign language. I wouldn't be too ambitious and go for the three and a half weeks or the pill. I'd never been any good at French at school, so it would have to be the full three months for me ...on the other hand I had studied the language for five years, even passed a CSE in it. That should cut down the lead-time a bit. Say two months.

I started 'Learn French in Three Months' in January 1976 and finally laid it aside in September 1992. I must have waded my way through it half a dozen times. It saw me through 'O' level, 'A' level, and nearly up to my diploma exams. It's a very comprehensive work but I reckon I know it all now ...except some of the twiddly subjunctive bits. I all but love that book. We've been through a lot together. I can fault it on only one point: its title.

Learn French in three months?

Twaddle.

The English say that English is the most difficult language in the world to learn - those who haven't tried to learn any other, that is. It's true that we have more words than anyone else and foreigners get confused by the wealth of idioms we use from a bewildering number of sources ('on a sticky wicket', 'kissing the Blarney Stone', etc). But we don't need to learn grammar. That monster only shows its teeth - adjectives, adverbs, pronouns, agreements and so on - when we come to learn a foreign language.

Grammar is difficult, dry and dull as ditchwater. Verbs for Example. English verb endings don't change much; 'Help', for instance, has three other endings, 'helps', 'helped' or 'helping'. That's because we use auxiliary verbs like 'would', 'could', 'might' or 'may'. The French do not; it's all done by the verb ending. Consequently 'aider' has thirty-six possible endings. Grammar! Simply reading (or writing) about it is enough to make one glaze over.

The French would have you believe that theirs is a logical language. Then why do objects have a sex? And if they must have a sex, why should a beard be feminine and a handbag masculine? Why should a thumb be feminine and a finger masculine? What are we to make of the fact that 'le livre' is a book, while 'la livre' is a measure of weight? Are the French of the opinion that men read while women get fat?

The French are, bien sur, sexist. While their language has different words for 'husband' and 'man', 'woman' and 'wife' are simply 'femmes'. While 'boy' and 'son' are each worthy of a word, 'fille' has to suffice for both 'girl' and 'daughter'.

The French curse English for its pronunciation. If you tell a Frenchman that 'rough', 'bough' and 'cough' do not rhyme he will not be impressed. He will shake his head in disbelief if he learns that the act of 'reading', must be pronounced differently from the town of 'Reading'. If you tell him how we pronounce 'Lieutenant Colonel' he will be deeply shocked, while explaining to him that there are two ways to pronounce 'bow', 'row' and 'sow' is likely to give him an attack of the collywobbles.

But it's not all one way. The French have their moments too: ville is pronounced 'veel' while fille is pronounced 'fee'. They stick 's' and 'd' and 'c' and 't' on the ends of words, then don't bother to pronounce them. Pourquoi? What is the correct way to pronounce 'en un an' or 'oie'? Who is 'tu' and who is 'vous'?

All this takes some learning. Years. So how do the 'quick' language courses justify their claims? I suppose it all hinges on the definition of speaking a language. It may well be possible to learn how to ask for a coffee, and even tell the waiter that he has a big nose, within three months, but that is hardly a basis on which to have meaningful conversations.

The 'get fluent quick' industry are exploiting a basic human weakness: we don't like to admit to being stupid. The king may be in the altogether, but if everybody else can see his clothes we'd better see them too. And if it is commonplace to learn French in three months, he who declares that he cannot is a brave man ...or a fool.

It must be obvious from the above that I did not learn French in three months. I am not a satisfied customer. Have I claimed my money back?

...Well no, actually.

The diploma for which I was studying was to be the end of my belated school days. Of the four papers I would take, the one that worried me most was the 'background' paper. It would consist of answering three questions, two in English and one in French, on aspects of French life such as the economy, politics, culture and society. I was preparing hard.

LEARN FRENCH IN SIXTEEN YEARS.

Having got hold of the papers that had been set during the previous three years, I saw that three subjects came up time and again: the TGV (the high speed train), immigration and education. A composite question would have gone something like: "The money spent on the TGV could have been more profitably spent on the education of immigrants: what is your opinion?"

I prepared essays on these subjects, and eleven others for good measure. These I corrected with French friends, Doctor Marais and two 'femmes' (the reason women are generally better at languages than men is doubtless because the female ego is less tender than the male one). Then I began to memorise as many phrases as I could.

The scientist Eric Braithwaite was once asked what single change he would make for the improvement of the country if he were Prime Minister. He replied that he would double teachers' salaries.

In France the teachers ARE the government, or a good part of it anyway. A third of French Deputies (Members of Parliament) are from the profession. This has its drawbacks, not least of which is the stupendously long summer holidays (nine weeks) that they vote themselves. By the time the holidays are ended, the children have been away from school so long that they are nervous and fretful. It can be imagined what state the mothers are in.

On the plus side, the French take education very seriously. From the age of two any child can attend school full-time as long as he or she is out of nappies and clean. This is light-years ahead of the niggardly attitude of successive British governments towards free nursery education. Teaching posts are widely sought after, particularly in country districts where reasonable jobs are few and far between. Along with the doctor, the vet and the notaire, the teacher is one of the most respected members of rural society.

Alice and David's school reminds me of my own primary school days in Kirkbymoorside, a Yorkshire moorland village.

After the mysterious disappearance of Letitia's (a class mate of Alice's) KitKat, a dire future was predicted for the (undiscovered) perpetrator: "Vol un oeuf, vol un boeuf" was the form mistress's summing up. ("Steal an egg, steal a bullock.") Solid country law. I can just imagine one of the schoolmasters at Dotheboys' Hall, thumbs in waistband, shoulders back, delivering the same homily in a 'I-know-what's-what' Yorkshire accent.

The same feeling pervades French education generally. An interview published in a national newspaper in May 1993 with the 'Grand Mistress of the Women's Lodge of France', who is also the headmistress of a comprehensive, shows which way the wind blows:

> "One day a father came to see me to complain that his son had stolen some money from him. He was a poor, modest man. He spoke at length to his son who was being rude to us continually. I said to the father, 'I see that you talk to your son a lot but don't you think you should give him a good clout now and again?' The father said, Oh! ...yes. Then I asked him: 'Will you let me do it for you?'
>
> "A little astonished, he agreed. I got up and quietly gave the kid a good solid whack. The father was a bit shocked. The boy looked at me with alarm, but we continued the conversation and I can assure you that that child was the quietest in the school afterwards."

Being a kid in France can be tough. Not only are children little darlings, they are also trainee citoyens. The school day is long, from 8.45 to 16.45 (even for the infants) and children in country districts often spend long periods being bussed back and forth.

Sending two-year-olds to school for a full day seems very hard. Tots are tots whatever nation they belong to and it is not unusual at the start of term to see impossibly tiny mites in tears and clinging to their mothers' skirts at the school gates.

From the age of six, children are given homework and an individual pre-printed progress register (60 pages thick!). This covers over thirty subjects, ranging from behaviour in class through history, reading, writing, arithmetic and so on. They are marked twice a term on a scale from 'A' to 'E'. The book is sent to the parents who must sign it.

Another example of the toughness of the trainee Monsieur and Mademoiselle is the school trip. Two months after joining her school, Alice's class of seven-year-olds went off to the mountains for two weeks on a ski trip. Minus Alice.

The French love art and their appreciation of it starts early. Thus David's school gave an exhibition of the paintings that the children had done 'After Paul Klee', 'After Jackson Pollock' and so on. At five, David had the unnerving ability to identify paintings by Van Gogh (pronounced 'Van Gog' in France), having studied the artist at school. He also knew the full story of Van Gogh's ear and suicide...

Some of their knowledge is not so much unsavoury as downright dangerous. David's classroom - when he was five years old -boasted a colour poster showing thirty fungi with a description of each one. Three or four were poisonous, most harmless, and half a dozen prized for their taste. Possibly this was a sort of 'survival of the fittest' exercise, in that those who learnt to read young would be able to differentiate the deadly from the delicious.

School children are subject to fads in France, just as they are in Britain. For a long time everybody collected 'pins' little badges issued by shops, companies, pop groups and so on. The papers carried reports of 'Pin Junkies'; kids who had collected several thousands of the things and who were desperately appealing for more. Suddenly 'pins' were old hat. For a while, all the kids took to wearing miniature babys' dummies round their necks.

These little crazes pass. Playground games flow on timelessly and unchanging, sometimes linking us to a past otherwise dead; for example 'The Wolf' (a chasing game) and skipping rhymes.

Then there are marbles. The French should be proud of their marbles. In pre-decimalisation Britain the coins in our pockets linked us to the days of Victoria. The French school child's marbles may well be as old. They come in an amazing array of colours and sizes (a school boy listed fourteen different types for me without pausing for thought). My favourites are 'terres', balls of baked clay which must be donkeys' years old, pitted and scarred by ten thousand playtime contests.

Our small English family has, for good or ill, contributed a tiny grain to the life of the French playground. David has introduced 'Kiss Chase' to his school.

Although many aspects of the childrens' schooling triggered memories of our own childhood, the summer fair struck fewer chords. It took place in the playground. The headmaster presided over the 'spin the arrow' stall. Ann usually wins at this and insisted on giving it a go, a worrying prospect as the headmaster was holding the prize (a large and very live hen) upside down by the legs. Luckily she lost. Other prizes were piglets.

The piglets reminded me of a visit I had made to René some weeks earlier. He had made no immediate reply to my knock, I had merely heard a sort of muffled banging. I knocked again. After a moment I was commanded to enter.

Standing in the hearth was a soot-covered apparition. A delayed Father Christmas? No, it was René himself. He beckoned me to the chimney, indicated a short wooden ladder leaning inside (the hearth being the size of a small car), and pointed up. Ten feet above, in the back of the chimney, hung four smoking lumps of meat; the nice little piglets we had admired in the stockyard for the last few months.

I forbade wife and daughter to gamble for piglets. I had neither heart nor hearth for the business.

We did, however, win a ticket (not a prize but a ticket for a prize) inscribed 'Bon pour isos'. Isos? My dictionary gave me no explanation. David made up a little chant 'Bon-pour-isos' to the yobbish cadence of 'Maan-yoo-nited'. As that didn't help much, we asked. The ticket must be taken to the hardware shop and redeemed. For isos? Bien sur!

Down at the quincaillerie (hardware shop) we presented the ticket and were duly presented with two isos: intricate pieces of moulded green glass. We looked at each other. We looked at the objects. We looked at each other again. We looked at the objects from a different angle. We turned them upside down and nodded wisely. Oh yes, isos. We avoided the shopman's eyes... but he knew.

Isos, he explained, are isolators, that is to say insulators. The things you nail onto your fence posts to hang electric wires from, and thus keep your animals from straying (the French have a thing about electric fences). The assistant reflected. Perhaps les anglais had no use for isos. Well then! He presented us with an alternative. Two batteries. I never did pluck up courage to try to explain that they didn't fit anything.

The Christmas school 'do' was advertised to start at eight in the evening and in reality kicked off at nine. With children between the ages of three and eleven performing, the hour might seem rather late. It didn't worry any of them - except ours. (French children are used to staying up late. Rather than being left with baby-sitters while their parents have evenings out, they usually accompany them.) By the time midnight came around, not only were the kids asleep against our shoulders, we were nodding off too.

Religion, one of the few subjects that is compulsory in English schools, is forbidden in French state schools, so this was not a nativity play.

David's class - minus David (asleep) - acted a circus scene. The children were dressed as tigers, monkeys, etc. The standard of the production was exceptionally high. Their teacher provided a cassette tape she had compiled of circus music, fine stuff that rattled round in the head for days afterwards. Rehearsals had been going on for weeks and the costumes were first class. The French excel at the visual.

Pauline, the tiniest girl in David's class, turned out to be the star of the show. Dressed as a clown, she was to walk across a plank of wood resting on two chairs. To the accompaniment of a circus fanfare, she ventured out along the beam. And fell.

Again the intrepid mite (four years old) ventured forth. The audience was hushed. She got further this time. And fell again.

One more time.

You could have heard a pin drop in the hall. Half-way across, the tot wobbled, righted herself, then skittered the two or three steps to the other side. The audience erupted in applause.

To round off the show, the oldest class sang a song. Improbable as it may seem, it was 'Ten Green Bottles'. Then Father Christmas arrived and we suddenly cottoned on to why we had been touched for funds for the 'Arbre de Noel' for the past few months. The school wasn't making a bid for the biggest Christmas tree in Europe, the money was for presents for the children - and what presents!

David didn't mind being woken up when he found that Father Christmas had brought him a Wild-West train set with an engine that rattled and whistled and with a cowcatcher on the front. Alice was given two books, one of which was Usborne's 'First Thousand Words in English', which it turned out she'd asked for. A mistake I think.

If you were not brought up to French time, it takes some adjusting to. The children managed it. We adults found it quite impossible. Only once did we arrive late. The school function was supposed to start at twelve-thirty. We arrived ten minutes early, and were surprised to see dozens of cars already parked. Surprise turned to amazement in the dining room, where all the tables were occupied, and people had actually started eating. Had the French nation suddenly become punctual?

"You're late!" said Nellie, with whom we were sharing a

table.

"Not at all!" I remonstrated, pointing to my watch.

"Don't you read the papers?" asked her husband. "Summer Time started at midnight."

The clocks had gone forward the night before and foiled our English conditioning.

If teaching himself French had taken their dim father sixteen years, how did the children get on? We had heard all the tales about speedy integration, the apparently knowledgable "of course, in two months you won't be able to tell the English kids from the French." We didn't take such stock phrases at face value. There was rather too much at stake for that.

The move was probably less of a wrench for Alice. She had many friends in England but no-one special. I had been coaching her in French and she had been going to lessons with the Alliance Francaise at Stony Stratford, near our home. David had never been to school, nor did he understand French and he and his pal Thomas were all but inseparable.

Their first days at school were understandably awful. Neither wanted to be separated from their mother and thrust into a strange school where they could not speak the language. The following conversation between them (after a freezing day when the pump and electricity had both repeatedly failed) did little to reassure me:

Alice: "Whose idea was it to leave Great Horwood?"

David: "Daddy's."

Alice: "Then daddy's a fool."

Daddy was inclined to agree.

As for the merry chant of "in two months time, you won't be able to tell the English children from the French," it proved to be, like many another pre-packaged assumption, pure bilge. At the start of the autumn term we had almost as much trouble getting them into school as we had had on the first day. If my 'learn when you can' route to French took me sixteen years, the kids' total immersion course took roughly a year.

At least they were at the right age to learn grammar. Just. The French child is issued at the age of six or seven with the first of three grammar books he will study until the age of fifteen. One of the forty-six things on which a seven-year-old is assessed is the ability to spot subject/verb agreements. Another is the ability to "express himself in the immediate past, the immediate future and progressively to a past and future further removed". Back to the future.

Gradually Alice and David settled in and made friends with Charles, Samuel, Jean-Christophe, Alexandra, Marina, Letitia and the others. The fact that their teachers spoke some English was a great help to them at first. But more important was the pains they took to make the children feel at home and the kindness they showed. They were more than dedicated. They loved the children and it showed.

We became accustomed to waiting an extra five minutes at the school gates for Alice after her first year. She needed the time to visit and kiss her previous teachers before going home.

Thank you Madame Duduoit, Madame Lorault, Madame Geffroy, Monsieur Cossec and Monsieur Brochard.

LIGHTHOUSE AT BARFLEUR

The farmer and the notaire. A butcher's quest.
The Dream Seller's dilemma.
Buying property 'en viager'.

An English solicitor once told me that boundary disputes were the bread and butter of his business. Certainly they were profitable to Maitre Mauvais. I met him through a boundary dispute of his own making.

The agency had been contacted by an English couple who were buying a repossessed farmhouse through the notaire and wished to buy an extra field. As they spoke little French and the notaire no more English, the buyers wanted someone to translate at the meeting that had been arranged on site.

It was to be an unpaid commission. I, however, was eager to use French as much as possible and was quite happy to provide unpaid interpretation. Exams were looming. Translating documents, writing letters, filling in tax forms, making phone calls for stranded motorists and doing guided tours were all grist to my mill.

I met the English couple at the farm, where the owner, who I will call Monsieur Pomme, was busy making his cider. A flatbed wagon, pulled by a tractor, stood in the stackyard. On the flatbed was the grinder and apple press which would turn Mr Pomme's trailer load of apples into cider.

Monsieur Pomme stood in the back of his apple-filled trailer. With the aid of a long-handled wooden shovel, he rhythmically fed the fruit (and worms and bugs) into the maws of a grinder mounted high on the flatbed.

The resulting pulp fell into a piece of hessian which had been laid inside a shallow, square, wooden frame. When this frame was full, the hired help folded the hessian over the top of the pulp and laid another frame on top of the first one. Then Monsieur Pomme began shovelling again.

When five of the frames had been filled, the grinder was disengaged and the frames were winched along the flatbed and under the crusher. Then the crusher's mechanism was engaged. Remorselessly the iron plate descended, squeezing the juice into a wide pipe that snaked away to Mr Pomme's cider store and into one of his tonneaux (barrels bigger than a man).

Finally, the pulp was shaken out of the squashed hessian sacks and the process was begun again. Mr Pomme and his hired help fortified themselves from time to time with last year's cider. It was a delightful rural scene - which was quickly spoiled by the arrival of Maitre Mauvais.

Mauvais had the reputation of being a 'difficult' man, and it is true to say that he was not happy to see me. To be honest, I don't think he was discriminating against me personally: I don't think he liked anybody. At first the notaire ignored me completely and spoke directly to the buyers. This, as they did not speak French, was somewhat difficult for them. I translated. At this Mauvais became heated.

"Ce n'est pas necessaire Monsieur, je peux parler en anglais."

Fair enough. I had prepared a written list of questions for the buyers, and proceeded to read out the first one in English. Mauvais spoke a word or two and dried up. I repeated the question in French. Again he became heated.

Monsieur Pomme chose this moment to join in. Having one's home forcibly sold must be a very distressing experience and he had been reconciling himself with more cider. Now his antagonism to the notaire became obvious. I have rarely seen a notaire addressed with anything other than respect by country folk. But it was not 'Maitre' Mauvais to this farmer; instead, he used a number of interesting Norman farming expressions which were new to me.

"I will have you arrested, you scoundrel!" snapped the notaire.

This incensed the farmer still further. He made to swing at the official, who promptly put the width of his car between them. The two circled the car, Mr Pomme in a crouched position, feinting now and again, the notaire fearful but emitting a steady stream of legal threats. The potential buyers and the cider-making contractor looked on in some bewilderment.

As it seemed that matters were not going forward in a particularly satisfactory manner, I placed myself between the two men, persuaded the farmer to calm down, and drew the notaire aside. Mr Pomme disappeared into his cider store.

The notaire may have been grateful to me, or perhaps he felt that as he stood in physical danger it would be unwise to further alienate his sole protector. He had nothing against me personally, I understood, but he was doing the negotiation and the fees were to be his, not mine. As I was seeking to enrich not my purse but my vocabulary - which I was doing very successfully - I quickly put him at his ease. A few minutes later the owner reappeared.

The English couple indicated the field they wanted to buy. As the notaire had omitted to supply a map of the property,

I began to sketch out a rough plan but the transaction was no longer on the plane of logic (if ever it had been). I was in the middle of a feud.

"Ce n'est pas possible," exclaimed the notaire triumphantly, "it would cut across a right of way!" (France is in the process of repartitioning all its land to do away with agricultural rights of way.) The notaire took evident satisfaction in telling the farmer that such a partition would make his other fields inaccessible to him. Mr Pomme flared up again. Again the notaire retreated behind his car.

When I explained what it was all about, the purchasers suggested a simple alternative. They were perfectly prepared to allow Mr Pomme to drive his cattle over the land, right of way or no. Or, if that was not satisfactory, they would buy the field except for a strip at the edge which would allow the farmer to have access to his other land. The Geometre (official marker out of boundaries) would mark out the new boundaries and all would be well.

It was a perfectly commonsense solution that pleased everybody except Maitre Mauvais. The reason he had not wanted an interpreter was that he did not want the deal to succeed. Whether this was to open up the chance for endless profitable litigation, or whether out of dislike for the farmer or the buyers, I cannot say.

There are always a number of English who are considering moving permanently to France. The Divines were one such family. The fax that I was given about them was a copy of a letter that the agent in England had sent to them:

> "You will meet Mr Alan Biggins at the Hotel St Charles in Quelqueville. He will be waiting for you between 9.30 and 10.00 on Monday the 18th of May. I have explained the situation concerning Mr Divine's employment in a slaughterhouse. There are several slaughterhouses around this area, a large one in Quelqueville and another outside Autreville."

CONFLICTS OF INTEREST.

The Divine family, father, mother, son and daughter, duly arrived. Mr Divine drove a bright green Lada, which he had bought especially for the trip for a hundred pounds. He was a butcher from Birmingham who wished to move to France. It was the family's first visit to the country.

Their dream house would have (or have the space in which to construct) three bedrooms, and up to ten acres of land; maximum price thirty thousand pounds. They came armed with a sheaf of property details which I had posted to them. They were particularly interested in the Picot farm.

I knew the Picot place well. It was a long, low, stone farmhouse with a mass of lean-to's to side and rear. There were also three large barns. In the barn farthest from the house Mr Picot had drawn my attention to a scratched message recording the disenchantment of a farm labourer: "Peu du pain, point du vin" (not much bread, no wine at all). It was dated 1706.

Monsieur Picot's parents had lived in the house for sixty years, in which time it had not changed a great deal. The only facility that it possessed was a wooden 'thunderbox' in the garden, with a heart cut into the door. Charming, but cold comfort on a winter's night.

Monsieur Picot's parents had been jackdaws - and with their many barns and outbuildings they could afford to be. On my first visit, the house and outhouses had been jam-packed with the most amazing miscellany of French rural life of the last century. There had been three Father Time scythes, a large mounted grinding stone for knifes and tools, two horse-drawn ploughs, a horse cart and a cider press. There were also hundreds of wooden-handled tools and implements. I had no idea what most of them had been used for.

In the outhouses was crammed the war booty: German and American ammunition boxes, three radios (presumably wrested from wrecked tanks), helmets, and War Department jerrycans which were stamped with the dates 1943 and 1944.

In the hay-lofts and lean-to's were horse harnesses, linen

chests, two wooden wheelbarrows, milk churns, a litter for transporting reluctant pigs, two butter churns with their tiny inset glass observation windows, and of course the ubiquitous cider tonneaux (including a small one full of calvados).

You could have started a museum just by opening the doors. I bought a few things from the owner, little realising that all the rest was to be carted off for burning.

When Monsieur Picot delivered my purchases, he did so in typical Norman fashion; they were stuffed in his horse box. He brought his wife and daughter too. They arrived one evening. His wife presented mine with a great armful of flowers. Alice and David were given sweets. I got nowt. The Picots stayed for a couple of hours and we had a very enjoyable time.

Monsieur Picot, although highly educated (a lecturer in mechanical engineering), had lost none of his native Norman suspicion. He would never have approached an estate agent to sell his property but was quite happy to use one on the advice of his notaire.

But I am forgetting the Divines. The Divines wanted to live in the country, somewhere peaceful where there was no crime, a place where they could have a bit of land, raise a few animals and put down roots. After seeing the Picot place we went to a bar for a drink. They were very enthusiastic about the farm. I, on the other hand, thought that it was wrong for them. It was very isolated and Mrs Divine could not drive.

Selling French property had taught me very quickly that isolation and lack of transport were a potentially deadly cocktail. Obviously it was the Divines' choice where they lived but would it not perhaps be more sensible to be in, or near, a village?

They were dubious. The Picot house was just what they needed. It had nine acres - plenty of room to put some cattle on - and the setting was spectacular. From the top field Mont St Michel could be seen on a clear day.

"Maybe so." I was non-committal. "But this afternoon I'd like to show you some less isolated places."

"This afternoon?" Mr Divine looked at me in puzzlement. "The agent in England told me that you were going to take us round the slaughterhouses to find a job." As Mr Divine spoke, I remembered the fax that I had received. I sensed the hand of Nemesis.

Once, long ago, when I was a programmer at ICI Paints Division, the whole department was compelled to attend a lecture by a systems programmer (a breed notorious in computing for being arrogant and inarticulate). The subject was 'online applications'. The stage was set for a lecture of awesome boredom. The speaker did not let us down.

The systems programmer spoke from prepared notes, perhaps thirty sheets of A4. He dragged his way remorselessly through page after page. There was little evidence that he knew what he was talking about and less that he cared. His voice never changed volume or tone; it was colourless, flat, lifeless, monotonous, dry, dull, tedious, tiresome and wearisome. A magnificent performance.

As the lecture went on and on, a dark cloud seemed to settle over my brain. For some reason I had with me an orange. The urge to lob it at the speaker was all but overpowering. But I didn't. I couldn't. I was powerless. The thing was inevitable, to be endured: written in the stars before ever our earth began.

So, too, was the visit to Quelqueville abattoir.

The Divines had been thinking about France for years and planning this trip for months. For months they had dreamed of an escape to the country, of better surroundings and a better start, mostly for the children. They had recognised their dream house in the Picot farm and could afford it if they sold up in England. Now the only thing left was to visit the slaughterhouse at Quelqueville and find a job. Naturally they needed me to help. They did not speak French.

The slaughterhouse at Quelqueville has a large carpark. Mrs Divine and the children stayed in the car while Mr Divine and myself wound our way deeper and deeper into the huge windowless building until finally we found the reception area. I explained our mission to the receptionist. She did not bat an eyelid. Would we kindly fill in some forms?

The forms, requesting information about the applicant's last eight jobs, were a perfect example of French bureaucracy. Not surprisingly, Mr Divine had difficulty remembering that far back. Then there was the question of the precise nature of his occupation; Mr Divine was not a butcher but a boner - what was the French for boner? Again, while his specialisation was pigs, Quelqueville was a sheep abattoir. Was the French method of boning the same as the English? (No.)

"Of course, at the moment," he pointed out, "I'm not boning or butchering. There's not enough work at the abattoir. I'm working as a caretaker." I suggested that we left that fact off the application form.

Each activity has its own specialised language and my knowledge of that of butchery was limited. Nevertheless, after an hour the forms were complete. The receptionist scanned them briefly: "Unfortunately we have no vacancies just at the moment. However, I'll put these on file." She brightened as a thought struck her. "Of course there's always Autreville slaughterhouse. You must take your friend there."

From time to time Nemesis must be grasped by the shoulder, spun on her heel and given a sharp kick up the backside, Goddess or not. For me the tragi-comedy had gone far enough. Impatiently I asked the girl: "Given that my friend doesn't speak a word of French, how do you rate his chances of a job with you?"

She shrugged her shoulders charmingly (she was very pretty). "Vacancies come up from time to time." She repeated that we should try the slaughterhouse at Autreville.

But I was not having any: "If you're adding the application to a file, does that mean that you have French applicants too?"

"Ah oui, from time to time people visit us, just as you have, Monsieur, and register themselves. It is wise. Jobs do come up from time to time, if you're not registered, you won't get any of them. That is why you should take your client to

Autreville."

I translated for my customer. Mr Divine's face brightened. "That sounds good. What if we were to come over, get settled in, learn French and give my name time to get to the top of the list?"

The secretary, who spoke some English, nodded enthusiastically. I asked her how many applications she had on file. She bent her head below the level of the reception counter and slowly thumbed through the file. "There are one hundred and five of them, Monsieur."

"Well," said Mr Divine, "what should I do?"

I looked at my customer for a long moment before answering.

The Divines' enthusiasm was obvious. They had seen the Picot place and they had seen what it could become. They would clean out the old pond and keep ducks on it. They would clear out and mend the pig sties, cow sheds and rabbit hutches. They would put sheep in the top field and hens in the chicken run.

A hundred such projects lay ahead of them; but little by little, and by their own hard work, they would bring the old farm back to life. They would put down roots there and their boy and girl would have an idyllic country childhood. In those spacious and peaceful acres above Mont St Michel, their dream could become reality.

And yet this small farm in France was a great gamble for my customers. I seemed a nice chap, I had seen it all before, and I was English. Besides, they had no one else to ask. What should they do?

The risks involved in moving abroad are, of course, enormous. As an agent, one has a ringside view of the comings and goings, and I knew that many buyers sell again (or try to) within a year or two. Buying, for them, had been a very expensive mistake. Why?

A few weeks earlier, I had decided to turn my file on such subjects as taxes, doing business, and health, into a course on living in France. For that course, I wanted to pin-point the danger areas. So I did a survey to find out what the other British residents in Normandy thought.

I came up with more than fifty questions. What did the 'permanents' like? Dislike? What mistakes had they made? What difficulties had they had? What recommendations would they make to others considering the move? ...and so on. It was a time-consuming job finding out. I dare say Mr Gallup could have told me that people don't answer questionnaires unless you sit down with them but it was news to me.

The 'reefs' became clearer and clearer. There were twelve major ones which had claimed victim after victim. (Five of them were related to earning a living, four to buying property; the other three were health insurance, education and language.) Then there is stress.

The British Medical Council publishes a table which allows you to measure the amount of stress you have suffered during the past year. It lists various events, such as the death of a partner, changing a job and so on. These are given points.

You tot up the points to see whether you are near the danger level. Above that line, your health and personal relationships are at risk. Moving a lifestyle, a culture and a country takes one right up to the thin red line. So the 'reefs' are very dangerous indeed...

The Divines knew no French. Most people I had spoken to listed learning the language as a major difficulty. Indeed, the second most popular piece of advice I was given was that French should be learned before moving to France. With language, as with swimming, total immersion is not to be recommended for the beginner.

Language posed particular danger for people who bought isolated houses such as the Picot place. Rural France does not have the wealth of clubs, societies and evening classes that exist in Britain. Social life is largely based on the family and neighbours. If both are lacking, loneliness can be a serious problem.

As could be expected, those who wished to earn a living in

CONFLICTS OF INTEREST.

France often ran into trouble.

The Divines were right to be worried. I had not 'seen it all before'; but I had seen enough to know that if they bought the Picot farm they could expect to have problems with language and isolation. They were also extremely likely to have trouble with earning a living, education and health insurance.

Nor were these the only risks that they were running. If my survey was representative, a large number of people who had moved to France had suffered serious problems when buying. The Divines had met me for the first time a couple of hours ago. 'Nice chap' I might be, English I certainly was; but what reason had they to think me competent in the niceties of French law?

My customer was becoming impatient. "Come on!" he said, "be honest."

On one point, the 'permanents' I had talked to had been unanimous. When asked "Would you recommend a long-term let before buying?", all forty, those for whom it had been the right move and those for whom it had been a mistake, answered "yes". Between them, they had come up with twenty different reasons for doing so.

I faced a dilemma. If I did not sell to the Divines I would be out of pocket. If I did sell to them I would make thousands of pounds. They, on the other hand, were likely to see their dream become a nightmare.

...Be honest! I gently explained to Mr Divine about the waiting list for the job at the abattoir, about the survey, and about the reefs. I told him what I considered his chances to be. If he wanted to take the risk, his best bet was undoubtedly to rent. He was disappointed.

I was none too happy myself. Where 'perms' were concerned, I was, I had to admit, not the stuff of which dream-sellers are made.

Sometimes a conflict of interests can be even more fundamental than that between the Divines and myself. Recently the French press was full of the fact that a woman had reached the magnificent age of one hundred and ten.

One hundred and ten years! How the human condition has changed in the old lady's lifetime! She was born before cars, radio, television, the electric light, refrigeration, penicillin, female suffrage, the telephone and the aeroplane. Life expectancy was short when she was a girl. She had done well to get through her first twenty years.

One would expect such an occasion to be the cause for celebrations and telegrams from the great and the good. So, indeed, it was.

But the rejoicing was not, perhaps, universal.

Madame had sold her property 'en viager'. This is quite an attractive option for the elderly. The buyer pays the owner a monthly allowance. This goes on until the owner dies, when the property finally passes to the buyer.

Madame's was a small house which she had sold for an allowance of (in sterling terms) two hundred and fifty pounds a month. She had entered into the agreement at the ripe old age of ninety. For twenty years the purchaser has been awaiting a return on his investment...

THE BAYEUX TAPESTRY

*The Conquest. The White Ship at Barfleur.
The Anglo-Norman kings. Entrails. Huguenots.
English, Norman and Breton pirates.*

If one visits the Bayeux Tapestry, one could perhaps come away with the notion that William was righting a great wrong when he invaded England.

William's blood-claim to the crown of England - that he was the second cousin once removed of the king - was slight. In any event the fact that he was illegitimate would probably have disbarred him from the throne, as it was to disbar his own illegitimate grandson from it. His claim rests, then, on the oath that Harold is said to have sworn to him.

The story goes that Harold, ship-wrecked off the coast of France, was taken captive by a local lord and released into William's custody. Harold then swore that the crown would pass to William upon the death of King Edward. The oath was sworn on a casket full of holy bones (which some versions say had been hidden by an altar cloth). Thus the vow was sacred.

William, therefore, had every right to gather thousands of knights, invade England and divide the country amongst his companions. Even the Pope gave his blessing.

Did Harold swear an oath at all? Although the claim is supported only by Norman sources, and history is, as they say, written by the victors, the Bayeux Tapestry may well be telling the truth.

The tapestry seems to corroborate the story of the oath in a telling detail. It shows Harold looking crestfallen on his return to King Edward, as if he is excusing himself for what he has done. This ties in with the widely believed theory that Harold was William's prisoner and bought his freedom with the oath.

On his deathbed, King Edward named Harold as his successor. The nobles of England confirmed the decision. These facts seem to suggest that William was not Edward's, Harold's or England's choice. Which means that it is extremely unlikely that he was freely promised the crown.

If we accept that the oath was taken, and that it was made under pressure, the justification for William's invasion is feeble. What would have happened to Harold if he had not promised William the throne? Was not the use of holy relics to sanctify an oath obtained in such a manner blasphemous in itself? Even had the oath not been coerced, was England Harold's to dispose of?

Possibly these thoughts went through the Pope's mind before he gave his blessing to the invasion. He was, however, already angry with the English, for electing an Archbishop of Canterbury not of his choosing.

More important, perhaps, is a fact that I have never seen mentioned in English accounts, although the Norman historians make no bones about it. They point out that by 1066, with half of Italy in Norman hands and having been defeated in the field by them, the popes were becoming somewhat accustomed to submitting to the will of the wildmen from the north...

In the end, what is perhaps most interesting about William's claim is not as much its legitimacy as that he bothered to make it at all. None of that tide of invaders that had swamped

THE ANGLO NORMANS.

Western Europe for five hundred years - not the Angles, nor the Saxons, nor yet the Francs - had ever thought that their attacks needed other justification than success.

Times were changing. By 1066, statesmanship was becoming almost as useful as the axe. William's genius was that he was equally dexterous with both weapons.

William's armada, drawn up at Cabourg, was the greatest Viking fleet ever to put to sea: hundred upon hundred of the sleek longships that had spread terror along the coasts of Europe for two centuries and which no power had found the means to defeat. The difference now was that the Vikings had adopted the French language (although Norse was still being spoken in Bayeux, the most conservative and proud of the Norman towns). Leading them across the sea would be William's dragon-prowed ship, the Mora. As they waited for favourable winds their high wooden masts looked to one observer "like a wood in winter".

Perhaps twelve thousand soldiers and hundreds of horses waited to embark. The troops that William and his officers had to lick into shape were a mixed bag. The Duke had had trouble finding enough volunteers from Normandy itself, so he had recruited mercenaries from Picardy, Brittany, France and half a dozen other states and kingdoms. The army's unifying factor was the thirst for plunder.

The modern traveller gets annoyed if he has to wait an hour to disembark after the five or six hour crossing between England and Normandy. There are a dozen such crossings a day. William had to wait twelve weeks to cross the Channel.

During the whole of July and August his fleet lay at anchor. It wasn't the distance that posed the problem. A hundred miles wasn't far to a people who had sailed half the coastline of Europe to reach Normandy. It was the wind; the same north-westerlies that had foiled William's father's invasion attempt in 1031.

Finally, on the 10th of September the invasion fleet set sail. Then the wind died and they had to put in at Saint Valery. The strain on William was immense. He had no wish to do as his father had done and turn his invasion of England into a raid on Brittany. Day after day he watched the weather-vane on the church and waited for the wind to turn. His allies got bored and began to quarrel among themselves. Some drifted away.

William was not the only threat that England faced. Three hundred ships carrying the king of Norway and his army appeared off Scotland. There they were joined by Tostig, King Harold's 'traitor' brother. The joint force sailed on to Yorkshire, beaching their boats in the Humber. They met the Northern Earls, Edwin and Morcar in battle at Fulford, two miles from York.

Here I can add a mite of my own history. I lived in Fulford as a boy and had an evening newspaper-round there. The last house on that round was Fulford Hall. I would enter the Hall grounds through a great iron gate, cycle up the gravel drive, deliver the papers and leave by a tarmacadamed track.

Following that track saved me a good mile. It ran downhill, past a pair of abandoned Victorian houses which had once been servants' accommodation, out of the Hall grounds and through a water meadow. It was on this marshy land, hard by the river Ouse, that Edwin and Morcar fought Tostig.

Running through the meadow is an insignificant stream called Germany Beck. The defending earls must have put up a good fight, for the stream got its name through being choked by dead invaders. (The North Sea was at that time called the German Ocean and everyone from beyond it was reckoned to be German.)

In winter I would think twice before taking the short cut from Fulford Hall. I hated cycling past the empty houses and across the water meadow in the dark. The trees that formed an arch over the track moaned like lost souls when the wind blew through their bare branches. My only friend was the narrow cone of light that my bike lamp gave.

It was an eerie journey and sometimes, when the lane was

flooded, a wasted one. Then I would be forced to push my heavy, black, gearless bike back up the hill and past those watching houses. Sometimes my courage simply failed me. For one reason or another, I often turned tail and went back the long way, up the gravelled drive.

Edwin and Morcar turned tail at Germany Beck too, and Tostig entered York. Hearing the news, Tostig's brother, King Harold, marched north. The two armies met at Stamford Bridge on the 25th of September. Harold's victory was complete, Tostig and the King of Norway falling in the battle. Of the three hundred ships that had left Norway, only twenty-four returned.

Still the Norman fleet had not sailed. It was getting close to the end of the campaigning season. Finally, three days after the Battle of Stamford Bridge, William's armada put to sea.

Although his ship was separated from the fleet during the night, the Duke landed in Sussex on the afternoon of the following day. William called for the soothsayer who had predicted a safe crossing, only to be told that he had fallen in the sea and drowned. "He's no great loss," commented the Duke, to the laughter of his companions, "if he couldn't even predict his own death."

William did not stir far from the beachhead in Sussex, nor did he take needless risks. He did nothing on impulse. He knew that the English king, with whom he had campaigned in Brittany, was an impetuous man. His hope was that Harold (or the Norsemen if they had won the victory in the north) would come to him.

William's were Viking tactics. If he could win a battle at the beachhead the rest would come easily. If not, he would not have far to run to his ships.

Harold came as quickly as William had hoped. He force-marched his army, greatly weakened after the losses at Stamford Bridge, and minus the forces of Edwin and Morcar, two hundred miles in a week. Not even waiting for reinforcements from the West Country, Harold marched into Sussex.

Envoys met on the 14th of October. According to the Norman historians, Harold offered William money to leave. Danegeld. William countered by suggesting single-combat, which Harold refused. Harold was accused of cowardice by his brother, Gryth, and the two came to blows 'like stable boys'. Harold seems frequently to have been at loggerheads with his brothers.

The story of the battle is too well known to bear repetition. With Harold dead, William marched first on Dover, then followed the Thames westward, searching for a crossing. He found none at London, paused only long enough to burn Southwark, and passed on. He finally forded the river at Wallingford in Berkshire and marched south towards the capital, stopping at Berkhamsted to parley with the dispirited Londoners.

William was crowned on Christmas Day 1066 at Westminster. His soldiers outside the Abbey, mistaking the traditional English shout of acclamation for a riot, set light to the houses outside. It was a typically Norman reaction.

Risings took place against William in the South-West and in East Anglia; but it was his fellow Norsemen of Northumbria who caused The Conqueror his gravest problems.

In 1068 the earls Edwin and Morcar renounced the invader. They would have been wiser had they marched south with Harold two years earlier. William 'pacified' the north but it soon rose again, with the Norman garrison of five hundred knights being slaughtered at Durham.

The English and Danish kings of England had often had cause to fear Northumbria but it took a man as ruthless and brutal as William to effect a final solution. The king who had men flayed alive for mocking the trade of his grandfather the tanner was also a military genius. A most dangerous combination.

In the systematic genocide known as The Harrying of the North, one hundred thousand men, women and children are thought to have been slaughtered in Lancashire, Yorkshire and Durham. William adopted a scorched-earth policy, ordering that all crops be burned, all animals slaughtered, all houses destroyed.

"Nothing moved among the burned out villages," according to the historian Ordericus Vitalis, "save packs of wolves and dogs tearing at the bodies of the dead." There was not an inhabited village between York and Durham and the land lay uncultivated for nine years. Vitalis, a Norman and not normally critical of William, said:

> "I have been free to extol William according to his merits, but I dare not commend him for an act which levelled both the bad and the good in common ruin by a consuming famine ...I assert moreover that such barbarous homicide should not pass unpunished."

In the Domesday Book of 1086, manor after Yorkshire manor was described simply as 'waste'.

As a lad in Yorkshire, I remember hearing stories of "When Billy got lost on 't moors". As often as not the tale would be ended with the observation: "Ah sud ah laaked to 'a bin thar with mi bow and 'arrer." (Some survivors of the butchery fled to the Lake District, where they are said to have held out in the valley of Borrowdale, slaughtering Norman army after Norman army until at last they were left alone. The Westmorland shepherds still count sheep using the numbers of their Viking ancestors.)

The Conqueror had fought for a duchy and a kingdom; next he meant to conquer France and make for himself an empire. But he was sixty years old. He had always been overweight; now he was becoming extremely fat. Phillipe of France mocked him, asking when he was due to give birth. William, not one to take mockery lightly, sent message to Phillipe that he would arrive at Notre Dame with ten thousand lances for candles. He led his army into the Frankish kingdom.

The Conqueror met his end just as victory seemed within his grasp. It was in the sack of the town of Mantes, only thirty miles from Paris. With burning timbers falling all around, William's horse reared and threw him.

In life, William had as much justification for his deeds as men such as he need: he got away with it. He never worried himself overduly about the atrocities he had committed until he faced the possibility of having to account for them to a greater authority than himself. Only on his deathbed and in fear for his immortal soul did he repent:

> "I have persecuted England's native inhabitants beyond all reason. Whether gentle or simple, I have cruelly oppressed them; many I unjustly disinherited; innumerable multitudes, especially in the county of York, perished through me by famine or the sword. I am stained with the rivers of blood that I have shed."

William, who was buried at Caen, was survived into adult life by three sons. William Rufus, who succeeded his father as king, was hated by his subjects for his murders, pillage, torture and extortion. He was shot dead in the New Forest in a hunting 'accident' and buried without ceremony.

He was succeeded by William's second son, Henry, who took the precaution of keeping his only surviving brother, Robert Courtheuse (short socks), a prisoner. Robert was to spend twenty-eight years in Cardiff Castle before he died.

In the port of Barfleur, where William's flagship the Mora had been built, Henry was to know tragedy. Barfleur lies in the lee of the northern tip of the Cherbourg Peninsula. Through this small and now peaceful port flowed much of the traffic of the Anglo-Norman kingdom. It was there, on the 25th of November 1120, that occurred an event which changed the history of Normandy, England and probably the world.

Henry (the First) and his court arrived at the port for the trip to England. With Henry were his son and daughter. Because of the need to contend with shoals, currents, tides and the wind, it was always a dangerous crossing. Night fell early at that time of the year. A sailor named Thomas sought audience of Henry.

"Sire," he said, "my father piloted yours from Cabourg to Saint Valery, and thence to Sussex and the conquest of England. I claim the same honour. See, there is my boat, the Blanche-Nef, which I have prepared for you. I have decked her in white, not a plank in her but is seatight, nor a cord missing."

The King went aboard his own ship, but he entrusted the young nobility to Thomas of Barfleur. There were three hundred of them, heirs to the highest and most powerful families of the kingdom. The rulers of the future. The bishop of Coutances blessed the ship.

The two ships left together, Henry's boat pulling ahead of that of his son and daughter. Seeing this, the young bloods on the Blanche-Nef (the White Ship) demanded that Thomas catch up. They wanted to make a race of the crossing.

Thomas set the helm towards the north-west, letting the ebb-tide pull him towards a passage through the reefs. Both passengers and crew had had a good deal to drink and took great delight in the sport, urging the pilot to go ever faster to overtake the King. The manoeuvre seemed possible if the helm was set due north. It was a very tricky passage, but Thomas knew it by heart. Suddenly the wind dropped and the Blanche-Nef had difficulty in fighting the current. Night fell. Drunkenness and excitement made the crew lose all caution.

With a terrible crash, the ship ran onto the Quilleboeuf rocks. It went down immediately, amid the screams of the suddenly sober courtiers. The tide carried off the corpses. There was only one survivor, a butcher from Rouen called Berold.

"King Henry never smiled again" according to Wade, his chronicler.

Henry himself died 'of a surfeit of lampreys', i.e. stuffing himself with too many eels. A disgusting enough death one might think, but nothing to what was to happen to him afterwards.

In medieval times dead kings were divided up and bits distributed here and there. Henry had his tongue and entrails buried at Emendreville and the rest of him at Reading. (Saints fared even worse, with fingers, feet, hearts and so on distributed wholesale to the faithful. Many Catholic churches - for example the wonderful cathedral of Coutances - still have their cases of holy relics on show to the public.)

The Conqueror had only two legitimate grandsons. One died in the wreck of the Blanche-Nef, the other (Robert's son) of a wound received during a siege. Of William's stock there remained an illegitimate grandson, who was passed over, and a granddaughter, Matilda, who inherited the throne. She married a Plantagenet.

The French language that came to England with The Conqueror was to have a great influence on English. Very often we have two words for the same thing in English, one Anglo-Saxon, one French: which explains why English has so many more words than French. Sometimes language can be revealing. Our animals bear Anglo-Saxon names when alive; pig, sheep and cow, Norman ones when dead; pork, mutton and beef. It was the Saxon slaves who looked after the animals and the Norman lords who ate them...

The Anglo-Norman lands stretched from Northumbria to the Pyrenees. Parliaments were held wherever the king lay; Winchester, Caen, Nottingham, Falaise. The flag of the kingdom was the flag of Normandy - three lions. They remain the coat of arms of England and Wales to this day, as a glance at the cover of a British passport will show. Normandy's flag, however, has lost a lion: the Channel Islands. (The Normans and English sometimes call heraldic lions 'leopards' for reasons baffling to the layman.)

France never forgot that Normandy had been hers. When King John was asked to supply troops to defend the Duchy against them, he is said to have replied, "I can do nothing for you" and continued his game of draughts. Normandy fell.

King John's successors did not share his views. The English came back for their Duchy time and again. To the French they were the 'Godons' from their repeated use of the phrase God Damn (a habit we seem to have passed on to the Americans).

The Normans for long hesitated in their allegiances. Some, like the inhabitants of La Lucerne, sided with the English. The village was renamed La Lucerne d'Outremer (across the sea), a name it keeps to this day. It was in this village, in the summer of 1992, that I saw an old lady drawing water from the well and carrying it off in two wooden buckets on her yoke. The scene can not have changed greatly since 1346. It is possible, of course, that she was having trouble with her disjoncteur.

The English fought up and down the Departement, building themselves a fortress at Granville, a peninsula at the northern end of the bay of Mont St Michel. They dug into the rock on the landward side so that the isthmus became an island at high tide.

The English Trench can still be clearly seen from up and down the coast, a bite into the spur on which the fascinating old walled town stands.

Normandy was fought over until 1450, when Cherbourg, England's last Norman possession, fell. The French had a few old scores to settle with the Normans. As King Louis re-established control, he settled them. On the 9th of November 1469 the golden seal of the Duchy of Normandy was placed on a blacksmith's anvil at Rouen and smashed to pieces. Normandy had been a dukedom and a kingdom. Now it was a province.

A taste of those days can best be had in Dinan, a jewel of a city across the border in Brittany. Here are fairytale towers and battlements, medieval houses and crooked streets. On The Jeruzel, the narrow cobbled street that winds down to the bridge over the river Rance, one has only to close one's eyes to imagine the knights clattering to battle, chickens and cocks exploding from beneath their horses' hooves.

England's links with Western France continued after we had been definitively booted out, of course. Gore Vidal once wrote that the Pilgrim Fathers fled to America "not because they were persecuted in England, but because they were not allowed to persecute others." Maybe. We certainly welcomed Protestants with open arms. Our country was the prime destination for the one hundred and eighty thousand Huguenots who fled persecution in Normandy during the seventeenth century.

The refugees made up an eighth of the Norman population, and gave England many distinguished families (among them the Chamberlains and Greshams) and a mastery in banking, porcelain and glass. Some of Doctor Marais' family came to England in this wave.

It was, of course, merely a continuation of a movement that had been going on for centuries across the English Channel.

The traffic wasn't all one way. Opposite St Vaast, the joint English and Dutch navies defeated a French battle fleet sailing to invade England in 1692. Seeing an account of the battle which had been prepared by the older pupils at Alice's school and hung on the wall for parents' day, it was strange to see the English fleet described as 'the enemy'.

Migration westward has been a constant in Europe throughout man's history. When that movement continued across the Atlantic to the Americas, the great French explorers who vied with the British were often either Normans or those one-time inhabitants of our islands, the Bretons. British ships preyed on French and French on British. Whether these were privateers or pirates depended purely on whether they were stealing for the king's purse or for their own.

An interesting little taste of that rivalry survives even today. It is in the waxworks at St Malo, from which port many of the raiding expeditions must have set off. The waxworks has many 'tableaux vivants' of the 'pirates', with music and recordings (in French). One of these relates the tale of how a

THE ANGLO NORMANS.

French pirate captain meets his English equivalent.

"Why are you a pirate?" asks the Englishman.

"For money" says the Frenchman "...and you?"

"For honour" is the improbable reply.

"Ah yes," sneers the Frenchman, "each searches for that which he has not got."

An interesting nautical tale. In fact, you could, as our American friends say, 'tell that to the Marines'.

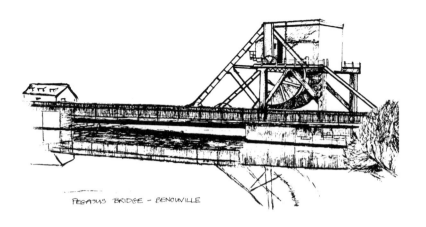

PEGASUS BRIDGE - BENOUVILLE

Allied preparations. The Atlantic Wall.
Deceptions. "A flock of seagulls."
Churchill's morning.

Many Britons associate Normandy first and foremost with
the D-Day landings which happened on the 6th of June 1944.
Where and when D-Day took place are, at most, only half of
the story. To see the landings in perspective, one must also
know why they happened, and how. They are questions that
those who lived during the War paid a high price to answer.

To understand 'why', the words of Winston Churchill can
hardly be bettered. On the 2nd of October 1940, the Prime
Minister of Britain's sombre, defiant and measured tones
were broadcast to the occupied peoples of Europe by the BBC

"Remember, we shall never stop, and never weary, and
never give in, and that our whole people and Empire have
vowed themselves to the task of cleansing Europe from the
nazi pestilence and saving the world from the new Dark
Ages. Goodnight. Sleep to gather strength for the morning.
For the morning will come."

To the few in Europe who heard the words, the speech
must have seemed madness. How could a country whose

army had been swept aside by the Germans in a matter of days - and which had left most of its equipment in France - presume to even face the might of Hitler's empire, let alone think of defeating it?

Didn't the British realise what they were up against? Belgium, Holland, Poland, Norway, Czechoslovakia and France had been over-run with startling rapidity. Russia was a German ally. Italy and Japan were casting their eyes over the British Empire to see what could be scavenged from it. The Americans had declared a policy of isolationism.

Why didn't Churchill face the facts? The Luftwaffe was swarming over the Channel. It outnumbered the Royal Air Force by three to one. The only thing that lay between Hitler and the total mastery of Europe was a handful of airmen. Air Marshall Goering had promised that he would sweep them from the skies within three weeks.

Hitler was prepared to be generous. He offered peace. He had, he declared, no argument with the British Empire. The British needed simply to recognise the nazi conquests and they would be left alone. It was no concern of theirs what the Thousand Year Reich did. To the victor the spoils.

Europe. What a glittering prize was Hitler's. Its resources were virtually without limit. The two million strong French army which was to be transported to Germany as forced labour would quickly be followed by tens of millions of others from the East. The industrial might of an entire continent would be turned to the demands of total war, for Hitler meant to betray his Russian ally, as he had betrayed so many others.

Hitler described nazi rule in Europe as 'The New Order'. Churchill called it 'The new Dark Ages'. The trainloads of state enemies - Jews, gypsies, communists, pacifists, homosexuals, the insane - who were already rolling to Hitler's death-camps would probably have agreed with Churchill. They too would be followed by millions of others. The nazis would clean up Europe.

That need not concern Britain. Hitler wanted only peace

with her. He had only one demand; the return of the colonies taken from Germany after the First World War. Churchill need merely accede to this 'final' demand and his people would be spared the destruction of their cities, the occupation of their land, and their own enslavement.

And so, probably, we would have been ...for a while. Instead, as the lights failed all across Europe, Churchill dared to speak of the dawn.

The preparation for that morning, which was given the code name 'Overlord', was, in Churchill's words, "the most difficult and complicated operation that has ever taken place". An assault against the strongest and largest empire ever to have existed in Europe. An empire which, expecting the attack, had had four years to build its 'Atlantic Wall'.

For the liberation to become a possibility, the Allies had to fight and win two major campaigns. The first of these was in the sky. The Battle of Britain was the curtain-raiser, saving Britain from occupation. The second campaign was at sea. This was won by the Royal Navy in the Atlantic. In ridding the sea of Germany's U-boat fleet and denying her surface ships access to it, the Senior Service broke the stranglehold on Britain and allowed convoys of arms and food to be delivered to Russia, which Germany had invaded in June 1941.

Then, in December of the same year, Hitler declared war on the United States, which had been supplying Britain and Russia.

The American colossus quickly showed its strength. Hundreds of airfields were built in East Anglia and the USAF and RAF pounded the Reich by day and night, forcing Hitler to commit his air force to defend his cities and industries. The American Mustang fighter in particular wrought havoc against the German air force. By June 1944 the Luftwaffe was but a shadow of its former self. It was no longer a decisive force.

Now, with sea and air virtually their own (at least for the moment), it was time for the Allied armies to liberate Europe, invade Germany and link-up with the Russians in the East. Preparations for that campaign went on even as the others were being fought.

The navy guarded the build-up of supplies from America and the British Empire; tanks, guns, food, aircraft and troops. The southern ports of England filled with shipping, while the land had been turned into a vast armoured camp. To give just one example, twenty-five square miles of West Devon between Appledore and Woolacombe had been evacuated of its entire civilian population to enable American assault troops to train. Millions of soldiers were billeted in tented encampments behind the coast.

The railways worked around the clock. Munition trains delivered seemingly endless consignments of bombs and shells to the vast ammunition dumps. Tens of thousands of trucks, tanks, railway engines, field-guns, bulldozers and other vehicles were gathered in marshalling yards ready for loading. The joke in England was that if the barrage balloons were unmoored from the south coast the island would capsize.

The Allies faced immense difficulties. The Channel would have to be crossed against an alert and watchful enemy and an assault from the sea made against Hitler's 'Fortress Europe', protected by what was probably the finest army in the world.

The four-year stalemate of trench warfare in the First World War had shown all too clearly the strength of prepared defences. Neither side had been able to cross No Man's Land. Millions of soldiers had perished there, as the endless lines of white crosses in the cemeteries of Flanders, and the lengthy war memorials in virtually every village and town of Britain, France, and Germany, sadly attested.

"What passing bells for those who die as cattle?
  Only the monstrous anger of the guns,
  only the stuttering rifles' rapid rattle
  can patter out their hasty orisons."
  (Wilfred Owen. Anthem for Doomed Youth.)

Now No Man's Land was between twenty-five and a hundred miles wide; the English Channel.

Colonel General Guderian, the German Inspector General of Armoured Forces, inspecting Lieutenant-General Bayerlein's Panzer (armoured) Division Lehr, based in Normandy, was almost contemptuous of the Allied threat.

"With this division alone," he told Bayerlein, "you will throw the Anglo-Americans back into the sea. Into the sea. Remember, your objective is not the coast, but the sea."

Panzer Division Lehr was reckoned to be the strongest in the German Army, and Guderian was an authority on tanks. He had masterminded the blitzkrieg which had over-run France in 1940.

The original Allied plan had been for a landing on three beaches. The British Field Marshall Montgomery, Commander of Allied Land Forces, insisted that five landing areas would be necessary in order to allow room for manoeuvre for the colossal numbers of men and vehicles. Eisenhower, the Supreme Allied Commander, was persuaded. Eisenhower, an American, was a man who modified his views according to circumstances and the views of others. He was also a good listener and a superb diplomat. He was the right man in the right place. Allied co-operation was to be excellent throughout the battle.

The two most favourable areas for the invasion were the Pas de Calais and the coast of the Cherbourg Peninsula. Both have superb beaches. Of the two, the Pas de Calais, just twenty miles from England, was the obvious choice. The Allies were keen that the Germans should believe that the attack would fall there, so they built hundreds of dummy encampments of plywood along the east coast of England (opposite the Pas de Calais) and generated thousands of radio messages between them. These were duly picked up by German detection units.

It was in the Pas de Calais that the German Todt (construction) organisation had made most progress with the Atlantic Wall. There, too, was stationed most of the German armour, six divisions as against two in Normandy.

The Germans, however, were also nervous about Normandy. Field Marshal Erwin Rommel, 'The Desert Fox', who had spent four years fighting the British Eighth Army in Africa, was posted there to bolster its defences. Rommel's view on the course of the battle was quite plain: "It is on the beaches that the fate of the invasion will be decided, and that within twenty-four hours."

He utterly lacked Guderian's confidence in the outcome. He confided to his staff officers: "If I were doing the invasion I should be at the Rhine in fourteen days." (Rommel often talked in terms of two weeks. In June 1940 he had written to his wife: "By my estimate the war will be won in a fortnight." But that was before the Battle of Britain, the Battle of the Atlantic, El Alamein, and the entry of Russia and America into the war.)

Even though the Allies faced enormous difficulties, Rommel had good reasons for his pessimism. His defences might look impressive; in the one hundred and thirty-six mile sector from the Cap de la Hague to Honfleur (in which the landings were made) there were eighteen hundred blockhouses. Had the Germans used the material to build a wall between the two points, it would have been a yard thick and nine feet high.

However, the Atlantic Wall in Normandy was less than a fifth complete. Some bunkers had no guns as yet, while many others housed captured weapons - which took over fifty different sizes of ammunition, some of them obsolete.

As for completing the planned defences - building the thousands of extra pillboxes, walls, tank traps and the like - the Todt organisation could not spare the men for the work. Rommel was forced to take his soldiers away from their defences and into the Forest of Cerisy for up to three days each week, to chop down trees and fashion wooden stakes to drive into the seabed.

The cement works at Cherbourg had closed due to lack of

raw materials and because of sabotage. A quarter of an ounce of sugar dropped into a concrete-mixer was enough to rob two hundredweights of concrete of its strength. The shield of a gun emplacement or the roof slab of a dugout might be sufficiently weakened to crumble like sandstone if hit by a shell.

Rommel was not getting much help from his own side. He had asked that two new types of pressure mine be sown in the English south coast ports. Admiral Doenitz had refused. If the mines were used, their secret might be discovered.

Rommel had also requested that a further thirty million mines be sown at sea. It was not possible. They could not be transported. Railways and bridges had been under attack from the air and from Resistance groups for weeks, and the transport system was in chaos. Those mines that did arrive could not be laid. A flotilla tried. All but one of the vessels was sunk by the Royal Navy. The last one turned tail and fled.

The list of Rommel's unanswered demands goes on. He had asked to be able to move the two panzer divisions at Caen up to the coast. The request was refused by Hitler. Rommel had also asked that these two divisions, the only tank forces in what was to become the invasion area, be strengthened by a further panzer division, to be based at Saint Lo. The request was refused by Hitler.

The Allies gave a somewhat higher priority to Normandy than the Germans. Their preparations were painstaking and methodical. Submarines had been landing small sections of men on the target beaches for weeks before the landings. These brave men surveyed the beaches for clay and soft sand, which would hamper troop movements, and reported on the defences. The plans of the Norman section of the Atlantic Wall were already in London, stolen by a Resistance worker two years earlier.

All the major landings in the Mediterranean had been made at nightfall but Overlord was to take place at daybreak. This was to avoid the mass of obstacles in the water, to give

the navy the oppo
to identify the bea

The first echelo
rising tide, so th
obstructions drysl
the German gun
assumption that t
The British had al
and specialised a

The landings w
bad weather on t
great distance tha
recalling units wl
ports the troops

A NORMANDY T

By mid-afternoon, 3,000
warships and thousands
south of the Isle of Wig
designated 'Area Z'
Circus.
"What Phili
and failed
attempt,
his me
Engl

Next morning came the fateful decision. Could the landings take place on the following day? General Eisenhower, on whom lay the responsibility for authorising the fleet to sail, was advised by his chief meteorologist, Group Captain Stagg, of a 'window' of better weather coming in from the west. On the basis of this, Eisenhower sanctioned the operation.

The invasion fleet sailed with gusting winds and six foot high seas. Some of the minor craft were driven back to port. It was a gamble; but had the force not sailed, then it would have had to wait a further fortnight for a full moon and favourable tides.

In one sense, the poor weather was on the Allies' side. The Germans judged it so bad that they had not bothered to station any craft in the Channel. Furthermore, the Luftwaffe had not carried out aerial reconnaissance of the English ports. Weak though the German air force was, this must still rank as a near miracle.

The fleet grew as more and more ships sailed out from Falmouth, Fowey, Plymouth, Salcombe, Dartmouth, Brixham, Torbay, Portland, Weymouth, Poole, Southampton, The Solent, Spithead, Shoreham, Newhaven, Harwich and The Nore.

landing craft, more than 500
of transports were massing to the
ht. The assembly point was officially
out was known to the navy as Picadilly

of Spain failed to do, what Napoleon tried
o do, what Hitler never had the courage to
e are about to do" signalled Commander Rich to
. Minesweepers had cleared ten channels between
and and France. On a front fifty miles wide the greatest
mada in history headed south.

Across the sea the Germans suspected nothing. Indeed Rommel had returned to Germany for his wife's birthday. He intended to put the trip to good use by persuading Hitler to transfer two more armoured divisions to Normandy. "The most urgent problem is to win the Fuehrer over by personal conversation" he noted in his diary.

Rommel's senior generals were at Rennes, a hundred miles from the coast, attending a course on the action to be taken in the event of an airborne landing. They could have learned from experience if they had stayed at their battle posts.

The BBC began to broadcast prearranged messages to the French Resistance, and advice to the civilian population on what to do in the event of air raids: "Leave the towns."

'Softening up' bombing had been going on for weeks from the Pas de Calais down to Normandy. Seventy-four German radar stations had been put out of action; only eighteen were still operational. Aircraft from England began flying a complex and pre-determined flight pattern over the Channel dropping 'window' (strips of tin foil) to fool the remaining radar stations.

The German screens were jammed. But it couldn't last. At 2.00 a.m., the operators realised that something was amiss. At first the technicians thought that the huge number of blips must be caused by some interference; there just could not be so many ships. Their commanding officer, Admiral Hoffman, ordered: "Signal to Commander in Chief West. Signal to the Fuehrer's headquarters. The invasion is on!"

In Berlin the Chief of Staff West scoffed at the reports. In this weather? "Maybe it's a flock of seagulls" he suggested.

He was not well informed. The first of the parachute landings had begun two hours earlier. Towards midnight two fleets of gliders had appeared over Normandy. They were to secure the flanks of the landings, on the rivers Douve and Orne.

Gliders landed on the banks of the Orne at midnight and British paratroopers quickly seized the bridge at Benouville (since renamed Pegasus Bridge in honour of the paratroopers' flying-horse cap badge). Moments later the troops took the bridge-keeper's house, the first house to be liberated in France. The operation went without a hitch. Major John Howard's men had been practising for weeks on a mock-up of the bridge.

Other bridges were targeted for destruction. It was vital that German tanks should not be allowed to get near the landing beaches.

At one bridge, on the river Dives, a German sentry of the 2nd Battalion was patrolling. He had every reason to curse the bridge. Four weeks previously, the neighbouring 3rd Battalion had organised a night exercise without warning the guards. The sentry, of course, could not have known that the shots that suddenly came from the approaches to the bridge were blanks. He had thought the balloon had gone up in earnest and opened up with his machine gun. There had been several wounded and two men killed. There was a terrible rumpus and some very unpleasant investigations.

All that flashed through the mind of the sentry on the bridge when, shortly after midnight, he saw three men with blackened faces charge up the embankment. "Silly fools!" he called at them contemptuously. He was given no time to call out or scream. Without a sound he collapsed, stabbed by a long paratrooper's knife. Five minutes later the bridge was blown sky high.

Forty miles to the north, American paratroops were preparing to seize the Vire and Douve crossings. This was in the area of the Carentan Marshes, where Virodorix had fought his doomed battle against the Romans two thousand years earlier.

Over the centuries the marshes had been partially drained; but Rommel had taken the precaution of reflooding them. Seventeen thousand men fell from the sky or landed by glider, many of them straight into the marsh. Much heavy equipment was lost and hundreds of men were drowned. Rommel's 'asparagus' - the stakes he had ordered to be driven into the ground - impaled countless gliders. It was a disastrous beginning.

Meanwhile, in England, the main aerial attack was taking off. It took the massed aircraft two and a half hours to cross London.

As dawn approached, nine battleships, twenty-three cruisers, one hundred and four destroyers, seventy-one corvettes and countless flak ships began to pour fire into the German defences. The guns of the warships were firing across the landing fleet. The noise of the barrage was deafening and continuous as sailors in thousands of turrets slammed home and fired an endless supply of shells. An impenetrable box of steel sealed off the invasion coast from supplies and reinforcements.

Hundreds of landing craft detached themselves from the main fleet and edged towards the beaches. Thousands of troops prepared themselves as best they could for the assault.

This was what the conquered people of Europe had prayed for since 1940. Churchill's morning had come.

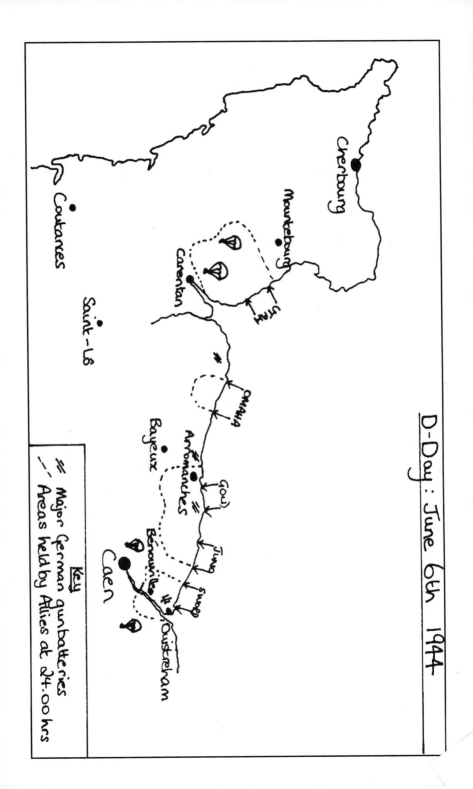

GUNS AT LONGUES SUR MER

The landings. The build up. The fall of Cherbourg.
Caen, the bloody battle. Breakout.
The death of Panzer Group Lehr.

The 6th of June 1944. A date that will echo across the centuries. Dawn. Bracketed by an arc of fire, and with a thunder that forced the ships' gunners to gape open-mouthed in order to stop their eardrums from being shattered, the greatest naval assault force in history moved out of the darkness towards the beaches of Normandy.

What were the thoughts of the defenders as the dawn revealed to them the seemingly endless armada, the work of hundreds of dockyards, tens of thousands of workers, the product of the two greatest maritime nations on earth?

Goebbels, the German Minister of Propaganda, had declared the defences to be impassable. "Let them come!" he had said. "It is what the Fuehrer wants: the Allies delivered on a plate." Many of the younger soldiers believed him. They had been programmed to do so for years. Hitler was Germany's Messiah. He was the greatest general of all time. The Allies could not pass.

Some of the older troops (and many of the defenders of the

Atlantic Wall were in their forties and fifties) were more cynical about their leader. This was not their first war. They saw this dawn as the inevitable consequence of their failure to conquer Britain. Judgement Day.

And the attackers? They had been on board ship for at least two days, some (especially among the Americans) as long as five. Many were seasick and had little further ambition than to reach dry land.

Some felt a sense of unreality, as if they had become trapped in a Hollywood movie. Most felt fear. A survey of a batch of British junior officers several weeks earlier had shown that the majority of them expected to die in France, as had most of the young officers in their fathers' war.

Because of the flow of the tide through the English Channel it would be high tide on the western-most beach, Utah, forty minutes earlier than on the eastern-most beach. Therefore Utah, in the American sector, saw the first landing.

Utah was the most lightly defended beach on the Normandy front, for the Germans thought it unlikely that an attack would come in front of the flooded areas; although here, as everywhere, Rommel was pushing for defences to be improved. A month earlier he had inspected 'W5', a blockhouse complex overlooking the beach, and insisted on seeing the hands of the officer in charge, Lieutenant Jahnke. Only when the commander saw that the lieutenant's hands had been cut by handling barbed wire was he satisfied.

Lieutenant Jahnke did not expect the invasion that day, and certainly not at low water. The sea goes out a long way around the Cherbourg Peninsula. Why the attackers would have to cross half a mile of sand. Half a mile!

It was 5.40 a.m. when Jahnke saw the ships. The ships! Ships beyond number; cruisers, destroyers, frigates, sloops, torpedo boats, assault craft, flak ships, gun ships, tank-landing craft, infantry-landing craft. Over the fleet flew thousands of barrage balloons. Naval barges with banks of rocket mortars began to launch missiles at Jahnke's strongpoint. Gunboats were firing continual salvoes.

Despite desperate resistance - including ordering a neighbouring gun crew to bombard his bunker to kill the American attackers who were on top of it - Jahnke's position was overwhelmed. (The bunker is now a museum.)

Twenty-three thousand Americans landed at Utah on D-Day with 'only' one hundred and ninety-seven casualties.

Things were very different at 'Bloody' Omaha, the second of the American beaches. Here three factors conspired against the troops. Firstly, their beach commander had refused the specialised armour that was used on the other beaches. Many of his troops were to pay for his omission with their lives. Eisenhower was to say later:

> "Apart from the factor of tactical surprise, the comparatively light casualties we sustained on all beaches, save Omaha, was in large measure due to the success of the novel mechanical contrivances which we employed, and to the staggering moral and material effect of the mass of armour landed in the leading waves of the assault. It is doubtful if the assault forces could have firmly established themselves without the existence of these weapons."

The second problem at Omaha was that the Americans faced four miles of defences largely untouched by bombing. This was not by design. A force of three hundred and twenty-nine B24 bombers had been instructed to smash the strongpoints and silence the batteries with 13,000 heavy bombs. They were flying blind because of cloud beneath them. Bomb release time and the duration of flight had been calculated to the second. At the very last moment headquarters, fearful of hitting their own troops, delayed the bomb release by a few seconds - and 13,000 bombs missed their target.

The third of the factors which was to make Utah such a

bloodbath was that there were twice as many troops defending the sector as the Americans had been led to expect from Resistance reports. This, as we shall see, was not the fault of the Resistance.

The result was four and a half thousand casualties. A dead or badly wounded man every six feet for four miles. Pinned behind the barbed wire on the rising tide, the Germans picked them off with ease. By the end of the morning, the American commander was considering abandoning Omaha.

The Americans had luck in only one respect at Omaha: the defenders' reserve could not launch a counter-attack, having been pulled back to oppose other parachute landings. (When the Germans reached the landing sites, they found that they had been tricked. The 'paratroops' were dummies which exploded on landing.)

The impasse was finally broken by the troops pinned on the beach. A brave lieutenant stood up and asked: "Are you guys going to stay here until you're dead?" and advanced on the barbed wire entanglements, blowing a way through. Followed by others, he wormed his way through the minefields.

Individual acts of American heroism such as this slowly overcame the defences, but at a terrible cost.

The central landing beach, Gold, was British. The only serious response to the naval bombardment was from four six-inch guns at Longues sur Mer, north of Bayeux - the Chaos Battery. These, like several of the batteries along the cliffs, were naval guns.

With their first salvo the Chaos guns straddled the ship carrying the corps commander and headquarters of the attacking force. The six-inch guns of HMS Ajax replied. Other ships joined in. The duel was over in twenty minutes. Three of the four bunkers had their guns silenced, two of them by direct hits through the loopholes.

'Direct hits through the loopholes' may sound rather sensational but a naval battery designed to fire at targets at sea does not have the usual fire slit. It must be able to traverse and be raised and lowered. The 'loophole' is about the size of a barn door - about twenty feet by ten.

The armoured steel plates to protect this gap had been dispatched from Germany, but never arrived. They were probably at some bombed-out rail junction.

The guns and the emplacements of the Chaos battery still survive at Longues sur Mer, as does the observation platform. The concrete blockhouses are the best preserved anywhere along the coast and the most evocative. They are pockmarked by shells, few of which have done serious damage to the thick concrete with its bracing of steel mesh.

The first of the four guns is completely destroyed and unrecognisable but the other three are just as they were after the duel. You can put your fists through the holes made by the shells that finished them off.

One wonders at the bravery of those gunners shooting at the hundreds of approaching ships while one after another of them was silenced, and at the skill of the gunners out at sea who managed from a range of several miles to lob shells right onto the guns.

The defenders were 'expendable' men. Some weeks earlier, Rommel had complained to Hitler about the lack of mobility of his troops. "Their role is to stay in their fortifications and die behind their guns," the Fuehrer had said, "so they don't need to be mobile."

The thorough training and steady nerve of their crews bought the first waves of landing craft onto Gold Beach with minor casualties; although three of five landing craft of 47 Commando hit mines.

The specialised armour proved its worth. Flail tanks cleared a passage through the mines on the beach, while other machines lay steel mats across the patches of clay. Bulldozers smashed through barbed wire and stakes, and filled craters. Strange mechanical monsters thrust ramps against the sea walls.

Behind the attacking troops the tide rose quickly. Within

an hour the outer obstacles stood in seven to eight feet of water. One of the strongest German strongpoints, at le Hamel, was taken at four in the afternoon.

The fourth beach, Juno, was taken by Canadian troops. By now the coast is getting more crowded, a kind of ribbon development that runs along to the ferry port of Ouisterham.

The Canadian landing was complicated by offshore reefs which meant that they had to come in towards high tide. This was what the Germans had designed the defences for; the tide covered the obstacles and the Canadians landed among mines and twisted steel. To add to their problems the troops landed before the armour, leaving the defences almost unscathed. Twenty of the leading twenty-four landing craft were lost or damaged.

However, the attacking troops were first-rate, and the pressure from the sea relentless. Other landing craft nosed past the wrecks; other men waded past the wounded and dead. A flak ship came inshore to engage one bunker. Infantry assaults cleared the beach. The coastal village of Bernieres fell by 9.30 a.m.

The final beach was Sword, a British assault. The seizure of the La Breche strongpoint at Lion sur Mer took three hours while troops coming ashore did so under strong fire.

Some of the men coming ashore were touched to see a French girl struggling in the shallows to help wounded men out of the water. Quickly the troops linked up with the Parachute Division that had taken Pegasus Bridge.

The defenders had been hit a shattering blow. Their resistance was uneven. Some strongpoints fought to the end. Others collapsed as Russian auxiliary troops simply ran away, bearing out fully a remark made by General Von Schlieben in a report some time before: "We are asking rather a lot if we expect Russians to fight in France for Germany against the Americans and British."

"You could see the Germans were really frightened because they were being so nasty." Said Nicole Ferté, a French girl at Herouville, two miles south of the Orne bridges. There was plenty to be frightened of as the wall of fire from the naval craft swept inland; as warships were rammed into the shore to make temporary breakwaters and piers; as wave after wave of landing craft hit the beaches; and as hundreds of Allied planes swooped on anything that moved.

The Germans bitterly asked each other the same question that the British and French soldiers had asked on the beaches of Dunkirk, four years earlier almost to the day: "Where is our air force?" By nightfall the Allied air forces had flown more than twelve thousand sorties over the beaches. The Luftwaffe had flown three hundred and nineteen, of which nearly all had been driven back or shot down. They claimed not a single Allied aircraft on D-Day.

The sky belonged to the Allies, and so did the sea. As the fleet had neared the Normandy coast, it had laid a smoke screen to protect the landings against the gun battery at Le Havre, which had survived a hundred bombing raids. During the day, three 'E' boats pierced the smokescreen. "It's impossible!" commented Heinrich Fromke, a rating on The Jaguar. "There can't be that many ships in the world." But there were.

The defenders, however, had an army; and a strong one. The strongest element of all were the two panzer divisions stationed near Caen. The officers on the ground begged that they be committed at once: without delay. The request was refused. The battle was being run from the Fuehrer's headquarters a thousand miles away and Rommel, the only man with both the ability to grasp the situation and the authority to get his assessment accepted, was away from the front.

Finally, the urgency of the request was appreciated and permission granted. At two-thirty in the afternoon, General Marcks told the 22nd Panzer Regiment's commander, Colonel Von Oppeln-Browinski: "Oppeln, if you don't succeed in throwing the British into the sea we shall have lost the war."

Oppeln set off with ninety-eight tanks. A handful of the machines reached the coast between the British and Canadians at Luc sur Mer, but they were too late. The Allies had been given precious hours to consolidate. Anti-tank guns engaged the German tanks and blew them up one after another. Without reinforcements, and finally without ammunition, they were forced back.

By nightfall the bridgeheads were slowly widening. Arromanches, site of one of the Mulberry harbours and now home to a D-Day museum, fell to the British by 9.00 p.m. There was still a seven-mile gap between the Canadians and the British, both the American beaches were isolated and the situation at Omaha uncertain; but no beach had failed. There was cautious optimism. The Canadians had made the most progress. They were within three miles of Caen, one of the targets for D-Day.

The following day, Bayeux, the first major French town to be liberated, fell to the British. Bayeux had been taken by the 50th Division as Rommel, newly returned from Germany, angrily informed General Bayerlein:

> "The 50th Division, Bayerlein! Our very special friends from Africa! We shall suffer the same fate as in Africa. Instead of the Mediterranean we shall have the Rhine - and we shan't get anything across! Get them out!"

The resulting panzer attack failed.

The situation was rich in irony.

Bayeux had been the birthplace of the Norman dynasty, its crest being one of the lions that are in the coat of arms of both England and Normandy. It is also the home of the tapestry depicting the Norman conquest of England. The 50th Division which had liberated the town was from Northumberland, descendants of the men who had slaughtered five hundred

157

of William's knights at Durham and of the Normans who had in turn 'pacified' the north.

The soldiers who had taken Bayeux were subjects of the English sovereign, one of whose titles is to this day 'Duke of Normandy'. The two opposing army commanders - English and German - were both of Norman stock. Montgomery's family 'came over with the Conqueror'. Rommel's were Huguenots who fled during the Catholic persecutions.

English soldiers were fighting once more for Normandy. But this beachhead into France was like no other in history. It was not an attempt to carve an empire, but to free a continent. The irony did not escape the men. The memorial they raised over the graves of their dead companions reads: "We who were vanquished by William have liberated the Conqueror's homeland."

(The Bayeux Tapestry itself spent the latter part of the War in Paris, in the Louvre. Some weeks after D-Day, Himmler ordered four SS officers to seize it and take it to Berlin. However, the Resistance had risen openly against the Germans. They seized the Louvre a few minutes before the Germans got there. The SS officers went away empty-handed.)

The battle developed slowly. The German soldiers fought stubbornly and bravely. They were greatly aided by the bocage. The narrow lanes with their high banks, thick hedges and small fields, made ideal defensive positions against attacks by tanks.

Now came the build-up. Large ships are difficult to unload onto open and exposed beaches. During a storm they must seek shelter or risk being run aground. Harbours were needed to fuel the breakout. There was no chance of taking Cherbourg quickly, and the Germans would certainly have wrecked its port installations. So the Allies were bringing their own prefabricated harbours, which were given the strange code name of 'Mulberry'.

The day after D-Day the first sections of the Mulberry Harbours were towed across the Channel at an average speed of four miles an hour.

Churchill called D-Day: "The most difficult and complicated operation that has ever taken place." The story of the Mulberries alone would have been worthy of the description. The harbours represented 15,000 man-years of work. Each consisted of 60 block ships to be sunk to provide initial protection from wind and water, 146 concrete caissons, four miles of breakwater, 22 pier heads and ten miles of floating roadway.

To ferry the materials to build two ports (each of the capacity of Dover) across seventy miles of sea, and then assemble them under the very noses of the enemy, was an undertaking on an unprecedented scale.

On the 18th of June the outer floating breakwaters were finished and the inner permanent ones almost so. The floating piers were half-finished. The roadways had been dispatched the day before and were half-way across the Channel. A fierce westerly storm blew up, the worst June storm for forty years. All of the roadways in transit were sunk.

The storm raged for three days and nights. Ships were dashed ashore onto the beaches of Normandy, while convoys in passage were driven back to England. By the 21st of June the Mulberries began to disintegrate - particularly the more exposed one in the American sector at Vierville. The floating breakwaters sank, the inner ones were breached, and the sea smashed through to destroy the sheltering ships.

The consequences were so serious as to imperil our very foothold on the continent. Indeed, the storm inflicted five times more damage than the Germans had done since D-Day.

The fact that the invasion took place at all in 1944 was largely due to American pressure. The British had urged caution, preferring to build up a great superiority in men and weapons. There is justification in thinking that had the invasion taken place earlier, it may well have ended in disaster.

If, however, Eisenhower had not given the go-ahead for the landings on the 6th of June, the next planned invasion date would have been during the storm. Then the landings would have had to be postponed until July, by which time the German V1 rocket offensive had started, and Rommel might well have had his extra panzer divisions.

New German weapons were coming into production: the world's first jet aircraft, electrically powered submarines, heavy rockets. By the end of the year three underground gun emplacements with barrels hundreds of feet long were scheduled to pour a thousand shells an hour into London and Bristol.

Between them the Allies got it right. However, all the conferences, compromises, arguments and accords could not alter the weather. The outcome of the Second World War could have been very different but for Eisenhower and the Allies' metrologist, Group Captain Stagg. That is how close a thing D-Day was.

The American Mulberry Harbour had to be abandoned after the storm. The one at Arromanches remained in action. Across it, a million men were landed on French soil in ten days, but the supply lines were dangerously stretched.

Cherbourg had to be taken as soon as possible. While the British and Canadians fought a bloody battle of attrition against Rommel's panzer divisions at Caen, the Americans broke out. With an initial American landing force of one hundred and thirty thousand men and another million to follow within ninety days, one hundred thousand vehicles and three thousand artillery pieces, they were a force to be reckoned with.

The German infantry, with no tanks, few aircraft and limited artillery support, were pushed back. At Carentan they were ordered by their leaders to hold the wedge between the American bridgeheads to the last man. Such tactics could only delay the Americans.

The only purpose of the Germans in the Cherbourg Peninsula was the defence of Cherbourg. Rommel knew this. Hitler did not. With his pathological desire to hold ground at whatever cost, he undermined all chances of holding the port. Time and again he intervened to forbid his troops to fall back. Even when he authorised withdrawal it was to be a fighting withdrawal, keeping contact with the Americans.

He designated Montebourg as the defensive line. It quickly fell, taking with it much of the ammunition, fuel and food which was to have been used to defend Cherbourg. The Luftwaffe tried to drop supplies at night but at least one consignment landed in the Channel Islands. Others contained, in the commander's words: 'nothing that can be used'.

On the 23rd of June, Cherbourg's defending General, Von Schlieben, reported to Rommel:

> "The enemy has broken through the land front and is advancing in four wedges. Hand-to-hand fighting is proceeding at some of our artillery positions and command posts. Navy considers harbour to have been destroyed for good."

The next day Von Schlieben was handing out iron crosses landed by parachute. The end was near. The Fort de Roule, a massive stronghold on the cliffs overlooking the port, quickly fell (today it houses a museum of the War).

Next it was the turn of the German Command Headquarters at Octeville. Inside, there was hardly room to swing a cat. Nearly a thousand men were sheltering in the subterranean galleries. The Americans dropped massive explosive charges into the air ducts and entrances of the headquarters. In the concrete tunnels, the defenders gagged on a nightmare cocktail of gunpowder, rotting cloth, exhaust fumes from the various motors, and sweat. The air conditioning system had failed.

The Germans fought back. On the 25th of June they shot down eighty aircraft with remotely controlled anti-aircraft guns sited on the breakwaters out at sea. The Americans retaliated by bringing up giant drilling rigs to bore holes into the headquarters complex. These were packed with explosives ...and ignited.

When Major Kuppers, the commander of the German

headquarters, was called on to surrender by the American Major-General Barton, Barton showed Kuppers a map on which the entire network of German positions was shown with absolute accuracy and in far greater detail than on German maps.

On the back were listed precise details about the types of weapons and ammunition at each emplacement and bunker, including the firing trajectories of guns not yet in place. Also on the map were the names of all strongpoint commanders and of the battalion and regimental commanders to whom they were responsible. On the next sheet was the area south of Cherbourg.

To his amazement Kuppers found that on this sheet, too, the German positions had been entered to the last detail. Even the number of troops in the different billets in the villages was correctly recorded. All command posts showed the names of their officers. Only one was incorrect. He had died two weeks earlier.

As usual, Hitler's order was to fight to the last man: "If the worst is to happen, then Cherbourg must fall into enemy hands only as a heap of rubble!" Faced with the choice between the pointless death of his men and surrender, Kuppers surrendered. It was the 26th of June. The forts in the harbour gave up two days later.

The destruction of the harbour facilities at Cherbourg was one of the most comprehensive demolition jobs of the War. It took three months to bring the port into partial service.

On the day that Cherbourg fell, the Germans estimated that 67 divisions remained in England. In reality there were 25. Incredibly, the Germans still believed that the mass of Allied forces had yet to be committed and would land in the Pas de Calais. To counter this non-existent threat, they held three times more troops and tanks in the Pas de Calais than they committed to Normandy. Thousands of other fresh German troops languished unused in the Channel Islands, an hour's journey from the Norman coast.

Hitler's command of the battle contrasts dismally with that

of the Allied generals. The launching of the German V1 rocket offensive only a week after D-Day was not against Normandy or the southern coastal ports, but London. (The offensive would have been much more terrible had London not been warned by the French Resistance of the location of nearly all of the launching sites, most of which had been destroyed.)

Hitler had complained after the First World War that the German army "was stabbed in the back" by the high command. By taking control of a battle that was taking place a thousand miles away, he condemned thousands of his own troops to defeat and death.

The Americans continued the assault. Now it was the turn of St Lo, a town built on a hub of roads between north and west Normandy. It was bombed to ruins. The scale of the damage can be judged from the cathedral which dominates the skyline, of which the towers have been reduced to stumps. There remains to this day an unexploded (defused) shell sticking out of the wall of the cathedral. Ninety-two percent of the town was destroyed.

The prison was destroyed along with the rest of the town. The hundred or so French Resistance workers imprisoned there would have doubtless perished in the raid if they had not all been executed by the Germans on the evening of D-Day.

Two weeks later, the brutal and bloody battle of Caen finally ended in victory for the Allies. Much of the city had been destroyed after very heavy bombing by the Royal Air Force. Group Captain 'Johnnie' Johnson was there, flying a Spitfire patrol. He noted in his diary:

> "Would the fiasco of Cassino in Italy, when the bombing attacks had created impassable obstacles to our own advance, be repeated at Caen? Was not the condemnation to death of many innocent French civilians unnecessary and a basic contradiction of the very principles we fought for? ...as I watched the terrible destruction

wrought on the French city, I could not help
wondering whether we were using a sledge-
hammer to crack a nut.

We were all aware of the military necessity to
break the enemy at Caen so that our ground
troops could eventually deploy into open country.
But we were not sure that this object could only
be achieved by the wholesale destruction of Caen
and the death of a great number of its inhabitants
...flying low on the fringe of the attack, I distinctly
saw a German tank thrown into the air, like a
child's toy, and turning over and over before it
fell to the ground."

Group Captain Johnson's fears were realised. Bulldozers
had to clear a path for the advancing armour.

Arthur Wilkes, an infantry man who entered the city after
the bombing, noted:

"My first thoughts on reaching the outskirts was
that the end of the world had come. Mountains of
debris towered twenty or thirty feet high, sewers
and service pipes had been blown to the surface,
cellars smouldered beneath the ruins. The dead
were everywhere."

The fatalities among the infantry were terrible on both
sides.
Montgomery's casualties at Caen were heavier than the
figure estimated by the British General Staff for the entire
campaign right into Berlin. Three quarters of British casualties
were from among the infantry, though they made up only
one seventh of the force. The casualties approached First
World War proportions.

"Normandy was a place were everything was
dead... we were bomb happy, always reduced to

three or four a section... I thought that if by some fluke I survived and got back to England there would be no young men walking about because they were all being killed or wounded in Normandy." (Leslie Cornwell).

British cemeteries ring the city.

Slowly the British and Canadians won the battle of attrition at Caen and pushed south. Meanwhile, the Americans were continuing to push down the peninsula. Materially, the Allies had an overwhelming advantage. The invasion had been superbly planned. PLUTO (a PipeLine Under The Ocean) had been laid across the Channel and along the length of the Cherbourg Peninsula to provide fuel for the armoured thrusts.

The factories of America were turning out tanks in their thousands, and they were being delivered promptly. The planning paid dividends:

"Provided the crews had been saved it was no great tragedy to see a hundred wrecked Shermans (tanks) lying about in the fields; one knew that another couple of hundred had just been put ashore." (Alan Moorhead)

For the Germans, movement of troops was all-nigh impossible during the day. The Allied fighter-bombers had complete mastery of the skies. In the words of one German soldier:

"Unless a man has been through these fighter-bomber attacks he cannot tell what the invasion meant. You lie there, helpless, in a roadside ditch, in a furrow in a field, or under a hedge, pressed into the ground, your face in the dirt - and then it comes towards you, roaring. There it is. Diving at you. Now you hear the whine of the bullets. Now you are for it.

You feel like crawling under the ground. Then the bird has gone. But it comes back. Twice. Three times. Not till they think they've wiped out everything do they leave. Until then you are helpless, like a man facing a firing-squad. Even if you survive it's no more than a temporary reprieve. Ten such attacks in succession are a real foretaste of hell."

Rommel himself was to fall victim to such an attack. He was thrown from his staff car with a broken skull. Afterwards his driver dragged him to the nearest village. The name of the village was Foy-de-Montgomery.

On the 30th of July the Americans burst into Avranches. The first American tank to enter the city is still there, a monument a hundred yards from the cathedral where Henry the Second did barefoot penance for the killing of Thomas a Becket.

The brilliance and dash of the American attack was due to General Patton. Scorning flank defences, he pushed his army across the single bridge over the river Selune at Pontaubault. Despite all the attacks that the Germans launched against this slender thread, Patton's army poured across in an unbroken stream of men, tanks, guns and trucks. Their momentum seemed unstoppable now, as they wheeled west into Brittany and eastward towards Paris. Breakout.

As the Germans' position became critical, they finally began the piecemeal movement of divisions from elsewhere in France. A German armoured counter-stroke from Mortain to cut the Avranches bottleneck was pounded to pieces from the air.

The British, Canadian and American pincers met at Falaise, birthplace of the Conqueror. (Strong contingents of Polish and French troops were also fighting with the Allies.) The Germans, ordered by Hitler to hold fast (as ever), were smashed by the Allied fighter-bombers, artillery, tanks and infantry. By the time they were authorised to escape from the trap, they didn't have a chance. According to Alan Moorhead, one of the War's greatest reporters:

"If I were allowed just one more despatch from this front this would be it; not because the despatch itself is important but because we have begun to see the end of Germany here in this village of St Lambert today.

The best of Von Kluge's army came here en masse 48 hours ago. They converged upon the village to fight their way out; long caravans of horses and gun carts, tanks and half tracks, hospitals and workshops, artillery and infantry. It was the sort of panzer battle array that the Germans have used to terrorize Europe for years. We knew no combination to stand against it.

And now here in the apple orchards one turns sick to see what happened to them. They met the Allies head on and they were just obliterated. Until now I had no conception of what trained artillerymen and infantry can do, and certainly this is the most awful sight that has come my way since the War began.

...It is exactly like one of those crowded battle paintings of Waterloo or Borodino - except of course that the wreckage is different. Every staff car - and I suppose I have seen a hundred - is packed with French loot and German equipment.

There is a profusion of everything: field glasses and typewriters, pistols and small arms by the hundred, cases of wine, truck loads of food and medical stores, a vast mass of leather harness. Every car is full of clothing and every officer seems to have possessed a pair of corsets to take home.

If you want a car you walk up and take your pick - anything from a baby tourer to a Volkswagen to a ten-ton half track... I say again I think I see the end of Germany here."

The Germans had lost a quarter of million men in Normandy. Some forty divisions were committed to the battle, leaving only skeleton defences. When they were defeated they had little left in France.

What of Panzer Division Lehr? - of which Guderian had said only three months before, "With this division alone you will throw the Anglo-Americans into the sea!" It met its end south of St Lo.

Two thousand American bombers attacked it in a sector four miles wide by two deep. That meant that each bomber had only to plough a furrow about ten feet wide. Which explained the appearance of the ground an hour after the attack; and the condition of the five thousand strong division. Over two thirds of the division had been put out of action, killed, wounded, buried alive or driven insane. Tanks and guns in the forward line had been smashed to pulp.

A second and third bombardment was made. The Americans found it hard to make progress on the ground. Not because of the defenders: they weren't much of a problem any more. The terrain itself had been turned into a lunar landscape of bomb craters, uprooted trees, wire and masonry. Tracks had to be cleared with bulldozers. Not a strongpoint remained. Merely a death zone.

The following day the German survivors somehow regrouped and resisted. They were attacked by four hundred bombers. The Germans retreated to Dangy, where Bayerlein was visited by a staff officer. Had he come with help? No, with an order. The Panzer Lehr was to hold out. No one was to leave their positions.

General Bayerlein stared at the officer. The man who had gone through El Alamein and had witnessed the collapse of the Afrika Corps without giving way was now at the end of his tether. His hands gripping the edge of the table, he spoke in a low voice, but his words hung heavily in the air:

"Out in front every one is holding out, Herr Oberstleutnant. Every one. My grenadiers and my engineers and my tank crews- they're all holding their ground. Not a single man is leaving his post. Not one! They're lying in their foxholes mute and silent, for they are all dead. Dead. You may report to the field-marshal that Panzer Lehr is annihilated."

The next day Bayerlein and his headquarters staff were trapped by American tanks in a house beside the Soulles stream. One by one the officers made a break for it. General Bayerlein was the last to go. He flung himself face down into a potato field as a tank shell came whining over. As dusk fell, he was seen walking down the road towards the town of Percy, alone.

PERCY CHURCH

*The battle for Percy. A Norman country town.
Madam I'm Adam. Vive la difference. Requiem.*

When General Bayerlein stumbled away from the wreckage
of his command, south along the darkening French highway,
he was walking a road that has been followed by soldiers for
thousands of years.

The General walked through a village on a crossroads;
Villebaudon. There he passed a cafe where a Resistance cell
had had its headquarters and a radio transmitter for contact
with England. No more. The Germans had surprised the men
at dawn two weeks earlier, lined them up in a field and
machine-gunned them to death. This was no 'Allo, 'Allo war.

A TOWN CALLED PERCY.

When Villebaudon was liberated by the British, it was little more than a mass of smouldering ruins. Then the Americans moved through the wreckage, fanned out into the countryside and began to descend the hill.

Less than a thousand yards ahead, on the left of the road, they saw a man waving something from a window of a house. Field glasses revealed that it was a tricolour. The man who was waving it was a refuge from St Lo. ("Leave the towns.") The Germans had seen the flag too. A few minutes later the house was in flames.("You could tell the Germans were frightened, because they started to get really nasty.")

After the War, a house was built to replace the gutted one, although you'd have to be an expert to date it; house styles tend not to change much in Normandy. The newer house stands at a little distance from the site of the original and is the home of a close neighbour. Monsieur Leseney is one of the people who drive past us as we walk the dog, and whom we wave to. One day he stopped, introduced himself and invited us round for a coffee.

The Leseneys are a charming couple. Monsieur told us about the refugee. Madame remarked, as we sipped her superb cherry brandy, that before that incident the Germans had been very 'correct': polite and well behaved. But not the SS; they were evil. They took away the Jewish lady who used to play the organ in the church in Hambye. She was never heard of again. She was blind. (Did she know what was to happen to her, the blind woman? Or did she, like millions of her fellows believe she was going for resettlement in the east? Probably. Few of the victims had any inkling of the depth of evil of the nazi empire - until it was too late.)

Madame Leseney remarked that unless one's country had been occupied, it was quite impossible to know what it was like or how you would react. Then she told us about the pigeon. The humble carrier pigeon did more than most to win the Second World War. In the Post Office at Villebaudon is displayed a war-time leaflet offering six hundred francs for each one handed in. German soldiers shot them down on sight.

The Americans at Omaha had three bits of bad luck: that their General refused specialised armour, that their bombs missed, and that there were twice as many defenders as they had expected.

This last was not the fault of the French. The Resistance worker who was surveying the area informed England of the doubling up of strength by sending off a message by carrier pigeon. In fact he judged the information to be so important that he sent off a second pigeon. Neither got through. By the time the third pigeon arrived in England the Americans were already ashore at 'Bloody' Omaha.

Nevertheless, enough pigeons did get through to allow the Allies to draw superb maps of the German dispositions at Cherbourg and many other places. Thousands of Resistance workers across France gathered the information. Some of them worked for the Todt organisation building the defences, others as servants, charladies, drivers. Some worked in organised teams, others, alone.

One of them was Madame Leseney's younger brother, a lad of twelve. He found a basket that had been dropped by the Allies. In it was a homing pigeon, one of the countless thousands that the Allies dropped in Northern France. The basket had a note on it, asking that the finder fill in a form giving details of the German troops in the area; the regiment, officers' names and so forth.

The boy's parents filled in the form and released the pigeon. They didn't give any details about themselves, of course, merely that they lived in Hambye. Nevertheless, they took a risk. The Germans shot more than a thousand resistance workers in Normandy and deported three thousand more, of whom less than half returned.

When the Americans came, they ranged their guns on Hambye but they didn't fire. Was it because of the carrier pigeon? Whatever the reason, Hambye escaped the destruction that was the fate of most of the surrounding villages.

A TOWN CALLED PERCY.

It was at Hambye that Mr Pouchin, a photographer for the local newspaper, the Manche Libre, told me of two Allied airmen. The first was Lieutenant Vezley from California, who baled out of his burning aircraft above the village and was hidden for seventy-five days by a French family behind the tonneaux in their cider store. The second was an English pilot, Sergeant Somerville, who crash-landed in the fields, could not free his jammed cockpit, and was burned to death before the eyes of a horrified but helpless farmer and his son.

On the main road between Villebaudon and Percy, on the opposite side to the 'new' house and out of sight behind the bed and breakfast place, is the site of the castle of the Seigneurs of Percy. The Percys marched away from their home one day in 1066, waited for months at Cabourg, crossed the Channel, fought at Hastings and fathered English children. They became the Dukes of Northumberland and now live in Alnwick. Their original home was burned down by the peasantry during the French Revolution. Only the gatehouse and moat remain.

A mile to the south of the 'new' house, the patchwork of fields and trees and hedges falls suddenly away, rising again to a wooded skyline several miles in the distance. It is a very green landscape, often misty. (In the lay-by overlooking the plain I did a fair number of corrections to this book, after first having dropped the kids off at school.)

The first thing to be seen of the town of Percy is the church tower. The visitor follows the road down the hill, past the incongruous pink Spanish-style villa (a survivor of the War) and into the town for which the Americans and Germans fought so hard.

Five thousand SS troops defended Percy. It was bombarded with twenty thousand shells from tanks, artillery and mortars. Much of the town was pounded to ruin. Then came the house-to-house fighting. While the soldiers killed each other outside, the population took what shelter they could in the wreckage of their homes. The town changed hands five times.

The Americans evacuated the civilians as soon as possible but not before more than fifty of them had been killed. A monument next to the church lists their names. I don't know how many Americans and Germans died in the battle. From the tales the locals tell, it must have been thousands.

Percy's church is unusual; a cathedral in miniature. Inside it there are a number of photographs of the town after the fighting; roofless houses and church. The structure of the church is itself a mute testimony to a hard-fought battle. From the steps upwards, chunks have been chipped and gouged out of the fabric by bullets and shells. The Germans used the tower as a platform to fire their mortars against the advancing Americans. The Americans responded by blowing them out of it with artillery.

Emile Zola could have been speaking of Percy when he wrote in The Debacle: "The gutted home was cast to earth, the ravaged field was blown with weeds, and Jean, humble and riven by grief, arose to make his way into the future; to the great and harsh task of a whole France to rebuild." (He could, in fact, have been speaking of half of Europe.)

Given the scale of the task, it's not surprising that many churches were not as beautiful after the War as they had been before it. The ugly cathedral front at St Lo, like the church at Villebaudon, was done as cheaply as possible. Percy's church fared rather better than most, although it has been surmounted by an unattractive concrete spire.

Opposite the church is an antique shop. In the window there is usually a portrait of General de Gaulle and a number of shell cases (war debris in varying stages of disintegration is a speciality in Normandy). Judging from the marks pitting the granite of which the shop is made, the old lady who owns it may have picked them up from the pavement after the battle.

Percy today is a fairly typical small Norman country town. It exists to serve the farming community. It has three agricultural suppliers, a maker of horseboxes, and a grain store.

Anyone eager to buy a tractor can visit two vendors, one at the north end of town, the other at the south. The one at the northern end offers a limited range of perhaps half a dozen machines, including a couple of those cabless red ones that have doubtless been taken in part-exchange and which never seem to die. It also stocks feeding troughs, fences and gates.

At the south end of town there is a choice of perhaps thirty tractors in red, blue and green, along with brand-new water-carriers. A wealth of hardware in primary colours is laid out along the roadside. These are the heavy armour of farming: harrows, crop sprayers, land-breakers, drills and combine harvesters.

Huge 'Elle et Vire' milk lorries crawl with painful slowness up the hills on each side of the town (although Normandy produces more milk than any other region of Europe, it is virtually impossible to buy anything other than UHT in the shops).

As everywhere in France, the locals read local newspapers, Le Monde and Le Figaro having only a small circulation outside Paris. Nearly everybody reads the daily Ouest France (which covers both Normandy and Brittany), or the weekly Manche Libre. Both these papers come out in regional editions so that one can generally be pretty certain to read about, or see a photograph of, somebody one knows in them.

The Manche Libre is where you look if you want to get a load of apples for cider making, or large quantities of betteraves (beetroots). You can also get your straw and your wood, either as logs or as 'three oaks to be cut up', through its 'small ads'. There are many reports of road accidents in the Manche Libre; but few of crime.

Although (or perhaps because) it has a huge gendarmerie and the police carry guns, Percy is crime free. The cars may well not be locked, nor the houses either. Cheque guarantee cards are not used. There is no grille on the bank counter. I don't suppose there's a burglar alarm in the town.

The quincaillerie where we were awarded our 'isos' is a

typically trusting place. Bulky articles such as wood, cement and breeze-blocks must be collected from its warehouse up the road. With the goods one is given a hand-written invoice which has to be taken back to the shop for payment.

Percy does not see many folk like our friend Adam. Adam has long blonde hair and would appear to have a death wish, since he is a 'BJ' and also parachutes from aeroplanes. He has itchy feet and is forever nipping off for six months or a year to exotic places, washing dishes, picking grapes or whatever. He programmes computers between trips.

When Adam visited us, he was on his way to Katmandu or some such place. When I showed him the sights of Percy - such as they are - we took with us a shopping list. As Adam studied the leeks in the grocers, a middle aged lady came in. In rural France the motto is 'toujours la politesse'. A newcomer to a shop will wish those present 'bonjour', and quite possibly a round of handshakes and kissings will follow.

"Bonjour." Said the lady. "Bonjour Monsieur, Madame." It gave Adam the chance to utter the immortal phrase: "Madam, I'm Adam." I bet he'd been waiting a long time to say that.

Adam, whose French is sketchy, caused a bit of a stir at the church. "I hope you enjoy your stay in Percy and find our church of interest" said the vicar amiably. Adam did not understand the courteous greeting. Instead of saying "I can only speak English" (which was what he meant) he replied: "Speak English!" The French are sensitive about the possible encroachment of English. Ordering them to talk in our language does not necessarily allay their fears.

Language can be a tricky thing, as I found out for myself when talking to a French family about the three bread shops in Percy. I said that French bread does not last long; because, I supposed, of a lack of preservatives.

I did not know the French word for 'preservatives', so took a guess that it was more or less the same as in English. The word was, as the French say, a false friend. Much tittering. The father tactfully corrected me. The correct phrase is 'agents de conservation'. 'Preservatif' is the French for condom.

Percy has a rather fine carnival. It only takes place every second year, so it is quite an event. The theme of the one we took part in was France. There were perhaps a dozen floats, each representing a region, Provence, Normandy, Brittany, Alsace and so on.

Alice was on the Basque float, kitted out in traditional costume. The French flair for the visual was shown in the floats. Each was decorated with thousand upon thousand of 'papillottes'; twists of coloured tissue-paper, built up into wonderful mosaic pictures of birds, people, country scenes and so on.

The roads were lined with spectators. The procession started late. It made its way along the main street and around the back of the town. There were four bands interspersed among the floats. Our neighbour René, who is (among many other things) a trumpeter in the Percy band, put his heart into playing 'The Fighting Temeraire': stirring stuff.

One of the floats in the carnival was from Rownhams, near Southampton, Percy's English twin-town. It was manned by recognisably English 'characters'; the plus-foured squire, the milkman, the bobby and the flowery lady with her tea service. And there was the vicar in his surplice, blessing the crowd while taking crafty pulls at a bottle hidden behind his bible (I'm not sure that this went down well in Percy).

The people of the twin towns often visit each other. There is a granite column outside the town hall at Percy. On it is a brass plate inscribed with the words: 'Rownhams 167 miles'. Rownhams, no doubt, has a similar signpost pointing towards Percy.

Visitors always remark on Percy's red British telephone box, which was donated by the people of Rownhams. The philistines of British Telecom have caused it to become a fairly major feat to have a 'proper' telephone box in Britain, never mind France.

The telephone box stands on the main road that runs through Percy. That road is called Liberty Highway. It was given the name as a tribute to the Americans who helped to liberate France. (Anyone who 'phones Britain from the red telephone box, or indeed from any telephone in France, is aware of the tribute paid to the thousands of British soldiers who laid down their lives for France. The dialling code is 1944.)

Bien sur, Percy is very different from its twin town. The traditional virtues of the French are the family, work, and France. I don't think they work any harder - or less - than the English, but they are certainly more outwardly patriotic. There must be quite an industry somewhere turning out tricolours.

The English visitor to Percy is far more likely to see the French flag than the French visitor to Rownhams is to see the Union Jack. As for the flag of England, if you were to ask the inhabitants of Rownhams (or any other English village) to describe it, I reckon that many of them would be unable to do so.

The people of Percy are much more conservative than their English cousins. They don't like change and they are reluctant to throw things away. These attributes are not confined to the French countryside. They are part of the national character. There is something to be said for French conservatism. For one thing, it makes for a stable society.

"Sometimes," Doctor Marais once remarked to me, "it means that we cling to things that were best discarded long ago." The most obvious example of this to the outsider is the 'priorite a droite'.

Priorite a droite (giving way to traffic joining a road from the right) is a profoundly baffling institution. It has been abolished on main roads and on some (but not all) roundabouts. It still exists in the towns (but not always) and minor roads (often). Some people abide by it. Some don't. The epitome of traffic confusion must be the roundabout in St Lo which also has traffic lights and priorite a droite.

The French tendency to 'hang on' contrasts markedly with the English one to 'get rid' (I will not presume to speak for the

Scots and Welsh). We have a tendency to search for novelty. Sometimes this is advantageous. It has given our country an extraordinarily rich record of innovation and invention.

Sometimes it means that we get rid of things which are in perfect working order. The urge to do so is built into our culture. The most obvious example of this to the outsider is in our system of registering cars. The number plate of an English car tells how old is the vehicle. It is a status symbol. The newer the car, the more important the driver. This practice fuels envy and jealousy and positively encourages waste.

Priorite a droite and English number plates have two things in common. Firstly, only the garage trade could defend either institution with any degree of conviction. Secondly, both are by-products of our national characters and our differences.

Now that we are part of 'One Europe', our leaders may be tempted to try to legislate away our differences. After all differences cause disagreements. Do away with the differences and the disagreements will disappear too. God help us if they succeed.

If this century of 'isms' and bulldozers has but one lesson to teach us, it is that pulverising the past does not provide a firm foundation on which to build the future. To enforce uniformity across national boundaries would have much the same effect on Europe as chain stores and concrete have had on our cities. Instead of the unparalleled richness of distinctive, sharp and individual cultures which we enjoy, we would leave to our children a 'Euro-purée' which would not merely be bland, but positively harmful.

No thanks! Vive la difference.

Percy does not claim to be special. If you stand by the church, however, the scene is worthy of a moment's reflection. Beneath the tower where the Germans died is a memorial to the people of this small town who were killed in the two World Wars. Here, twice a year, the people of Percy remember the cost of war. The town band is there. René waits to play. His face, normally creased in a smile, is serious as he recalls the bombs and shells, the fear, the pain, the death and the waste that he saw as a child.

Many must have stood in Percy and had more or less the same feelings over the last couple of thousand years. Normandy has often been a battlefield. Gauls, Romans, Britons, Francs, Vikings, Normans, English, Germans and Americans have all marched through this corner of France. Soldiers following orders, marching to conquest or defeat. Often they have been marching to, or from, England.

If the fates of Normandy and England have been interwoven since the dawn of history, we two are, of course, a corner of a greater design: Europe. Europe's story, too, is a bloody tapestry of conflict, combat and carnage. It has been fashioned at the whim of tyrants and dictators of all nations. Men whose element has been discord. Men with 'expendable' armies and bloody hands. Men whose lust for power and possession have led to countless millions of deaths and blighted lives.

Of all the European empires, the nazi empire was the largest, foulest and shortest lived. Tens of millions died because Hitler wanted Europe while Europe didn't want Hitler. But that blood-bath was only the latest in a series that has lasted since man first walked the continent. The latest and the last. The sixth of June 1944 saw not only D-day but a new dawn for Europe.

One Europe. The church tower and war memorial at Percy bear witness that force can never achieve that dream. The red telephone box on Liberty Highway is a hint that it may yet come about through friendship.

René raises his trumpet to his lips and salutes the fallen.

VILLEDIEU

Exam time. Britain and the Brownies of Villedieu.
The Iles Chausey. Exam results.

The months rushed by. I had prepared and presented my
course on living in France; now examination week was upon
me. I was to sit the exams in London, at a college near
Waterloo Station.

I have always preferred Shank's pony to the underground
(given the choice) and walked to the South Bank on the three
days of my examinations. London in springtime was a
delight. There was a vitality and purpose in the streets, and
an incredible diversity to which I had been blandly indifferent

when I had worked in the city.

Hidden away among the small streets of the capital were a host of specialist shops, beautiful buildings and small parks. For a few days I was like Mole in Wind in the Willows, as I caught scent of old haunts.

I realised for the first time how 'quaint' England was, with its red double-decker buses, its postmen on bicycles and its milkmen. I gradually became aware, too, of an odd mixture of English things that I had all but forgotten; sandwiches and cheddar, pies, pubs and parsnips. For some reason I had not forgotten the worst aspects of urban life, such as litter and traffic jams...

I reached the college. Waiting in the reception area were candidates from all over the country; we were like a camp of displaced persons, each clutching his or her briefcase or plastic bag. Some took out files for last minute revision, others got to talking. I listened eagerly. It was the first time I had met anyone who was to sit the exams - all my knowledge of what was to come was based on looking at previous papers.

My eavesdropping did not reassure me. A lot of people were resitting papers they had failed the previous year. My chances of getting the 'grand slam' of all four papers seemed remoter by the minute.

I got talking to a British Rail manager from the Midlands who told me that he often served as an interpreter in meetings with the French national railway. What he didn't know about the high speed train wasn't worth knowing. We compared notes with others. Nearly everyone had done the same as I - prepared essays on the high speed train, immigration and education, the subjects that had been set during each of the last three years.

At nine-twenty we entered the examination hall. A curtained stage ran across the front of the room. The Spanish exams were to take place here too, so I would have to be careful where I sat.

A dozen rows of ten or so old-fashioned desks (with

inkwells) were laid out, each with its steel and plywood chair. Rain was falling heavily outside and all the lights were on. It was oddly comforting. Examinations seemed not to have changed very much in the last quarter-century.

Watched by a hundred pairs of eyes, the minute-hand of the clock above the invigilator's desk jerked forward. Then came the measured tones: "You may start now."

I turned over the paper and skimmed through the questions. There was no question about immigration. There was no question about the high speed train. There was no question about education. I glanced around. It seemed to me that there were some very green faces. I turned back to the paper and went through it more slowly. Here was one I could tackle:

"It is essential for the economic future of France that farmers concentrate on productivity. What is your opinion?" My mind went back to a farmer in Gavray market: what had he said? "We will learn to worship the gods of efficiency and speed. Europe demands sacrifices. We will be the sacrifice... there will be eight beggars, one rich man and a thief ...it will be too late to remember our virtues when you have buried us."

I ticked the question and continued down the sheet: "Does the French Desert still exist?" I knew a bit about that too.

Then: "To what extent would you say that the traditional values of the French republic - work, family, France - are still alive in France today." France: the land of family, patriotism and tricolours.

I reached for my first sheet of paper.

After my exams I visited a friend who works for English Heritage. He had done well for himself. He had a huge office on the sixth floor of Fortress House, overlooking the city. Even here it seemed that I could not get away from Normandy. Two floors above and half a century earlier, Eisenhower had planned the Normandy landings. We went to the pub for a pint.

Back in Normandy, we attended the midsummer festivities at Villedieu les Poeles, 'God's town of the frying pans'. Villedieu is one of those rare Norman towns that were lucky enough to come through the War unscathed. It is a honeypot for the British, for it has a bell foundry, a clock museum and dozens of shops which sell copper. It was founded by the Anglo-Normans (or were we English by then?) as a staging post for the Crusaders between England and the Holy Land.

It is a fascinating town, built around a series of courtyards which once led one into another. Lots of little alleys still exist, running down to the river Sienne (not the Seine). There are many winding stairways, and tiny doors which show that people are taller nowadays and that the streets have been raised.

Villedieu is the home of Alice's Brownie troop, who were kind enough to invite Ann and I to give them a talk about Britain.

What would interest a typical group of French girls about our country? The Royal Family seemed a good bet. We dug out some postcards and books about them. British schools? We prepared a bit on them too. Pop groups? Out came the cassettes. Then there was 'Olde England'; postcards of Bath and Norwich and Exeter and Rye. National costumes; the kilt, the Welsh shawl, the bowler.

In the event we discovered that what really interests the French - or at least the Villedieu Brownies - about Great Britain is the Loch Ness Monster.

In Britain only three of the pre-Christian quarter festivals have been taken over by the church; Christmas, Easter and All Saints. We no longer celebrate the midsummer rites but the French do, as the feast of Saint Jean.

The Brownies' service was held in the open air. It began with a religious ceremony ("If you do not love God more than you love your mother and your father, you are not worthy of Him. If you do not love God more than you love your friends, you are not worthy of Him." French kids have to be tougher than English kids, even as eight-year-olds.)

The audience sat on wooden staging around the car park while the Scouts, Cubs, Guides and Brownies acted out scenes and played games from around the world - Phileas Fogg being the linkman. A burning brand was put to the kindling beneath the pile of thick logs in the centre of the carpark, and the summer fire burst into life.

Towards midnight the children were led out of the carpark and disappeared into the streets of Villedieu for a treasure hunt. Alice and David had adjusted to French time.

By now the annual flood of visitors was upon us. All our friends were welcome. The only drawback with our visitors was that they seemed to think that we were as keen as they were to see Mont St Michel or the invasion beaches. The first two or three times we were.

Mike and Liz and their girls Catherine and Jennifer (the same age as Alice and David) had a pretty miserable week of constant rain, so our planned trip to the Chausey Islands seemed debatable.

The morning of the trip started dry but there was no way of knowing if it would continue so. I consulted René. He wandered off to the foot of an apple tree. I thought that he hadn't heard me. He bent over, scooped something from the grass and returned. With a little smile, he opened his fingers. In the palm of his hand sat a brilliant green cricket, perhaps three inches long.

"He will tell us" the farmer said, giving the insect a little prod. The cricket jumped into the air. René smiled. "Voila. It will be fine today. If he had jumped onto the ground it would have rained." He was, as usual, quite right.

The Chausey Islands are the southern continuation of the Channel Islands - but quite, quite different. They are much smaller for one thing, the largest of them (the Grande Ile) being only about a mile and a half long by half a mile wide - and they have a permanent population of perhaps half a dozen. Granite from the islands was used to build Mont St Michel. Nowadays the chief industries are fishing and tourism.

They say that there are three hundred and sixty-five

islands at low tide and fifty-two at high tide - convenient numbers which suggest that they are impossible to count.

The port of Granville is the main French embarkation port for the Channel Islands as well as the Chausey Isles; a distinction that has not always been to its advantage. It was the last Norman town to be in the firing line during the War. The Allies did not bother with the Channel Islands (which Hitler had garrisoned especially heavily), leaving them to wither on the vine.

A few days before the end of the War, the German garrison sailed out of Jersey, attacked Granville, destroyed the harbour installations, killed several citizens and made off with prisoners. (Impressive German gun emplacements still stand on the headland at Granville.)

To board the boat for Chausey, we trooped down the worn stone steps from the quayside for fifty feet (it was low tide). Our journey was on a summer morning so perfect that it made me feel glad to be alive. It was as if the world had been scrubbed clean. The small boat bumped and bucketed through the water, its wash cutting a trail through an endless line of jellyfish. An hour later we landed at the quay of the Grande Ile. Lobster pots were piled on the jetty.

We strolled around the island, picnicked in a sandy cove and watched vivid green lizards darting among the stones of the breakwater. Then came the serious business of exploring the most impressive feature of the Grande Ile, its wrecks. There are perhaps a dozen of them, of wood and of iron, some probably a hundred years old. They have been driven far from the sea by tides and winds of unimaginable power. A better children's playground it would be hard to imagine.

In the cafe we admired the fish tanks full of lobsters. Alice and Catherine disappeared. They were gone for so long that we started to worry. The girls returned just as we were preparing to comb the island. They had been in the toilets when the disjoncteur had disjoncted.

At the tip of the Cherbourg Peninsula, facing out across the Channel, is the lighthouse of Barfleur. It has three hundred and sixty-five steps and fifty-two windows (though this time they can be counted). The lighthouse is a wonderful granite column over two hundred feet high which has faced the worst that nature has been able to throw against it for nearly two centuries. It can be climbed free of charge. Unlike most of the British lighthouses, automated and sadly empty now, it is still manned by a crew of three.

With its powerful beam and in a place which sees so much shipping, it is essential that this beacon be kept burning at all times. Would it be facetious to wonder if three is the minimum number of men required to hold down the disjoncteur?

The summer dragged slowly to a close. Both René and Therese had retired now, and Therese, to her great relief, was down to one cow, Connette, which she milked by hand. Our knowledge of wildlife grew. We discovered that the creatures who inhabit the stream are muskrats. "A present from the Americans." René wryly informed me.

At last the letter came with my results. Could I put away my grammar books and dictionaries at last? Might I allow my subscription to Le Point to lapse? Could I for the moment leave Le Monde, Le Figaro, Ouest France and The Manche Libre aside? Was my sixteen years of part-time slog ended at last? Was I finished with it all? Had I pulled off the grand slam and passed all four exams? Had I? Had I? Had I?

I tore the letter open.

I had passed the oral.

I had passed the general knowledge.

I had passed the essays.

...I had failed the translation from French into English. It was the exam for which I had done the least preparation - and I had payed the price. I had, I realised bitterly, overlooked a small but vital point. I had spent sixteen years chipping away at French - but for translation, English is equally important.

For my next attempt at the examination I have taken the precaution of borrowing Doctor Marais' copy of 'Learn English in Three months.'

THANKS.

I would like to thank:

My wife for her unfailing support.

Roger Ward, for his invaluable help and advice with this book, both editorially, and in design.

Peter Spooner for exhaustive (and exhausting) proof reading.

Martin Marix-Evans for technical assistance.

Eddy Frost and Cath Ward, for being guinea-pigs.

Keith Nelson for his patience and help.

And to:

La famille Grente.

Brigitte and Jerome des Bouillons.

Doctor Jean-Paul.

Marie Gaubier.

Merci!

ACKNOWLEDGEMENTS.

I would like to thank the following for permission to quote from the books mentioned.

Histoire de la Normandie Jean Mabire & Jean-Robert Ragache.
Editions France-Empire 1986

Caen, the brutal battle. Henry Maule.
David & Charles 1976

Overlord. Max Hastings.
Michael Joseph 1984

Eclipse. Alan Moorhead.
Hamish Hamilton 1946
(The estate of Alan Moorhead)

Wing Leader J. E. Johnson
Penguin 1959

Invasion-They're coming! Paul Carell.
Harrap 1962

The secrets of D. Day. Gilles Perrault.
Corgi 1965

The Battle of Britain. Edward Bishop.
George Allen & Unwin.

The struggle for Europe. Chester Wilmott.
Collins.

A NORMANDY TAPESTRY.

If you have enjoyed this book and would like to share your pleasure by giving it as a gift to a friend, further copies can be ordered directly from the publisher:

> Kirkdale Books,
> Spring Lane,
> Great Horwood,
> Buckinghamshire,
> England.

Price as per cover.
Please add £1.50 for post and packing.

Please state if you would like your copy to be signed by the author.